Exploring
America
in the 1980s

Exploring
America
in the 1980s

Living in the Material World

**Molly Sandling &
Kimberley L. Chandler, Ph.D.**

The College of William and Mary
School of Education
Center for Gifted Education
P.O. Box 8795
Williamsburg, VA 23187

Prufrock Press Inc.
P.O. Box 8813
Waco, TX 76714-8813
Phone: (800) 998-2208
Fax: (800) 240-0333
http://www.prufrock.com

Contents

Acknowledgement

Thanks to Pamela N. Harris, who acted as the editorial assistant for this unit.

Unit Overview

Introduction to the *Exploring America* Units

These humanities units will focus on the way in which the literature, art, and music of each decade reflect the history and events that were occurring in America at that time. These units are intended to stimulate student interest and creativity, to develop higher order thinking skills, and to promote interdisciplinary learning.

The units could be used as a supplement to a social studies curriculum or a language arts curriculum, or could be used as stand-alone materials in a gifted education program.

Introduction to *Exploring America in the 1980s: Living in the Material World*

Exploring America in the 1980s: Living in the Material World focuses on the energy and excitement of the 1980s as the economy improved and new technologies led to new opportunities, as well as the struggles of those who didn't share in the prosperity and the tensions that built over our global role. Topics included in the unit are:

» the literature and music that explored both the excitement and the fears of the new technology and prosperity of the 1980s;

» the music, art, literature, and photos that contrasted the wealth of the decade with the realities of a changing economy and growing Rust Belt;

» the changing immigration patterns of the 1980s and the art, music, and literature of the new immigrants;

» the effects of the escalating tension and gradual end of the Cold War in literature and music;

» the struggles in the inner city and continued inequalities;

» the effects and reactions to Michael Jackson and Madonna on the music and culture of the 1980s; and

» the music that explored the tension between our desire to help improve the world and our objection to military and government involvement beyond our borders.

Standards Alignment

Social Studies

This unit includes activities that address the National Curriculum Standards for Social Studies. Specifically, the activities relate to all of the 10 themes of the National Curriculum Standards for Social Studies: Culture; Time, Continuity, and Change; People, Places, and Environments; Individual Development and Identity; Individuals, Groups, and Institutions; Power, Authority, and Governance; Production, Distribution, and Consumption; Science, Technology, and Society; Global Connections; and Civic Ideals and Practices.

English/Language Arts

This unit also includes activities that align to these Anchor Standards of the Common Core State Standards in English Language Arts:

» CCSS.ELA-Literacy.CCRA.R.1: Read closely to determine what the text says explicitly and to make logical inferences from it; cite specific textual evidence when writing or speaking to support conclusions drawn from the text.

» CCSS.ELA-Literacy.CCRA.R.2: Determine central ideas or themes of a text and analyze their development; summarize the key supporting details and ideas.

» CCSS.ELA-Literacy.CCRA.R.4: Interpret words and phrases as they are used in a text, including determining technical, connotative, and figurative meanings, and analyze how specific word choices shape meaning or tone.

» CCSS.ELA-Literacy.CCRA.R.7: Integrate and evaluate content presented in diverse media and formats, including visually and quantitatively, as well as in words.

» CCSS.ELA-Literacy.CCRA.R.9: Analyze how two or more texts address similar themes or topics in order to build knowledge or to compare the approaches the authors take.

» CCSS.ELA-Literacy.CCRA.R.10: Read and comprehend complex literary and informational texts independently and proficiently.

Overarching Concept

The overarching concept for this unit is *identity*. This concept can help students to understand events, music, art, and literature during the 1980s. The unit explores the decade, giving students multiple opportunities to analyze events based on a developing understanding of how the idea of identity applies to specific situations. The conceptual approach also allows students the opportunity to make comparisons to other time periods, thus developing a deeper understanding of the generalizations about identity and when they may or may not apply.

The first lesson in this unit introduces the concept of identity. Teachers may wish to conduct an activity based on Hilda Taba's (1962) Concept Development Model prior to teaching the first lesson. Students are asked to brainstorm examples of identity, categorize their examples, identify "nonexamples" of the concept, and make generalizations about the concept. The following generalizations about identity are incorporated into this unit of study:

»   Identity changes with new ideas, experiences, conditions, or in response to other expressions of identity.
»   Identity is created by a group, person, or outsiders, and self-created identities may be different from how others see one's self.
»   There are multiple elements of identity and at different times, different elements have greater or lesser importance.
»   Although members of a group or society may have different individual identities, they still share particular elements of identity.

Identity is integrated throughout unit lessons and deepens students' understanding of social studies and a given historical period. Students examine the relationship of important ideas, abstractions, and issues through the application of the concept "generalizations."

Curriculum Framework

Concept Goal

Goal 1: To understand the concept of identity in 1980s America. Students will be able to:
»   describe how the American identity changed during the 1980s; and
»   describe how changes in American identity in the 1980s were revealed in the music, art, and literature of the decade.

Process Goals

Goal 2: To develop skills in historical analysis and song and artwork interpretation. Students will be able to:
»   define the context in which a song or piece of art was produced and the implications of context for understanding the artifact;

» describe a writer's or artist's intent in producing a given song or piece of art based on understanding of text and context;

» consider short- and long-term consequences of a given document or artifact; and

» analyze the effects of given documents or artifacts on the interpretation of historical events.

Goal 3: To develop analytical and interpretive skills in literature. Students will be able to:

» describe what a selected literary passage means;

» cite similarities and differences in meaning among selected works of literature; and

» make inferences based on information in given passages.

Content Goal

Goal 4: To develop an understanding of historical events occurring in the United States during the 1980s. Students will be able to:

» describe major historical events during the 1980s that affected the American identity; and

» describe music, art, and literature of the 1980s that reflected the American identity.

Assessing Student Learning

Teachers should assess student progress based on the quality of individual products and achievement toward the goals of the unit. Question responses should be assessed based on demonstration of insight and ability to use text to support inferences. Writing activities should be assessed based on understanding of the social studies content, and may also be assessed for clarity and insight as desired. Oral presentations of completed work should be assessed based on coherence, content, and clarity of the presentation. Teachers may provide rubrics for students related to the required assignments or work with students to develop rubrics for assessment.

Teaching Resources

Recommended History Books

These history textbooks are recommended for providing supplementary information about the historical background of the events described in this unit.

Appleby, J. (2010). *American vision*. New York, NY: Glencoe/McGraw Hill.

Cayton, A. R. L., Perry, E. I., Reed, L., & Winkler, A. M. (2002). *Pathways to the present*. Upper Saddle Ridge, NJ: Pearson Prentice Hall.

Davidson, J. W., Stoff, M. B., & Viola, H. J. (2002). *The American nation*. Upper Saddle Ridge, NJ: Pearson Prentice Hall.

Kennedy, D. M., & Cohen, L. (2012). *The American pageant*. Boston, MA: Cengage Learning.

Useful Websites

- » *American Experience: Eyes on the Prize*:
  http://www.pbs.org/wgbh/amex/eyesontheprize
- » Learning to Give philanthropy education resources:
  http://learningtogive.org/
- » Library of Congress Civil Rights Resources:
  http://www.loc.gov/teachers/classroommaterials/themes/civil-rights
- » Library of Congress Song and Poetry Analysis Tools:
  http://www.loc.gov/teachers/lyrical/tools
- » National Park Service, Historic Places of the Civil Rights Movement:
  http://www.cr.nps.gov/nr/travel/civilrights
- » PBS Learning Media, Civil Rights:
  http://www.teachersdomain.org/special/civil
- » PBS Makers: Women Who Make America:
  http://www.pbs.org/makers/home
- » Rock and Roll Hall of Fame Education:
  http://www.rockhall.com/education
- » Smithsonian Folkways:
  http://www.folkways.si.edu
- » Teaching Tolerance:
  http://www.tolerance.org
- » VH1 Music Studio:
  http://www.vh1.com/partners/vh1_music_studio/

Implementation Guide

This guide assists the teacher in implementing this unit in his or her classroom. It also includes background information about the instructional models utilized throughout the unit.

Guidelines

The following pages offer some general suggestions to help the teacher implement the unit effectively.

Support for Teachers Implementing the Unit

It is important for teachers implementing this unit to read it in depth before beginning instruction. Conferences and training workshops sponsored through the Center for Gifted Education (CFGE) can help teachers understand the core components of the unit and provide informal tips for teaching it. Customized professional development, including comprehensive curriculum planning for incorporating this humanities series, is also available. Please contact the CFGE at cfgepd@wm.edu for information about professional development options.

Suggested Grade Levels

Exploring America in the 1980s was designed for use with high-ability students in grades 6–8. Although the unit was developed for middle school students, some components may work well with students at other grade levels. Caution should be exercised when using the materials with elementary-aged students, however, as some of the music and literature contains mature themes.

How to Incorporate the Unit Within the Existing Social Studies Curriculum

This unit is intended to represent 5–8 weeks of instruction in social studies for high-ability learners. The unit may be taught as core content, or it may be used as a supplement to the core curriculum. The unit is also appropriate for use in a seminar setting.

Implementation Time

In this unit, a lesson is defined as at least two 2-hour sessions. A minimum of 40 instructional hours should be allocated for teaching the entire unit. Teachers are encouraged to extend the amount of time spent on the various topics included in the book based on available time and student interest.

Materials

Availability of materials. Given that this unit focuses on the 1980s decade, the materials are contemporary in nature and have not yet become part of the public domain. In most cases, it is suggested that teachers make use of Internet resources whenever possible rather than purchasing the materials cited. Both Prufrock Press and the Center for Gifted Education have developed websites that include a list of resources and their respective URLs: http://www.prufrock.com/Assets/ClientPages/exploring1980.aspx and http://education.wm.edu/centers/cfge/1980s. Because URLs tend to change, these websites will be updated periodically.

Potentially controversial materials. This unit focuses on the trends and issues in 1980s America. Some topics being discussed and some of the materials being used may be controversial to some students and parents. It is crucial that teachers preview all of the materials prior to teaching the unit and determine what is appropriate for their own schools and classrooms.

Teachers should always read the literature selections or listen to the musical selections before assigning them to students and be aware of what the school and/or district policy is on the use of materials that may be deemed controversial. Although many gifted readers are able to read books at a significantly higher Lexile level than what other children their age are reading, content that is targeted at older audiences may not be appropriate for them.

☐ Made original, insightful contribution(s) to discussion?
☐ Extended or elaborated on a classmate's ideas?
☐ Used evidence from the text or another student's comments to support ideas?
☐ Synthesized information from discussion in a meaningful way?
☐ Posed questions that enhanced the discussion and led to more in-depth understanding?

Student comments: _____

_____

_____

Teacher comments: _____

_____

_____

Figure 1. Participation checklist. Adapted from Center for Gifted Education (2011).

Assessment

This unit includes both formative and summative assessments, which are found at the end of each lesson plan. Because discussion plays a prominent role in the students' learning in this unit, teachers may want to consider teaching students a specific process for the discussion elements and develop tools for assessing student participation. The Socratic Seminar is one method for organizing discussions. (See http://socraticseminars.com/socratic-seminars/ or http://www.readwritethink.org/professional-development/strategy-guides/socratic-seminars-30600.html for additional information.) Or, the teacher may want to design a checklist, such as the one in Figure 1, to give to students to keep track of their contributions during discussions. The students can check off the criteria as they meet them. Using this checklist, the student and teacher can monitor the student's participation in various discussions.

Teaching Models

There are five teaching models that are used in the unit to facilitate student achievement toward the unit objectives. Teachers should familiarize themselves with these models before beginning the unit.

The models are designed to promote discussions in various settings. The teacher should determine the best way of organizing students for discussion in order to facilitate student understanding and appreciation for the variety of answers that are given. These teaching models also provide students with the opportunity to support their responses with evidence from the literature or other resources. Multiple perspectives can be shared and encouraged through appropriate use of the models. The models also may be used to prepare students for a discussion in another content area or about a current event. Students can complete the models in a whole group, in small groups, or individually before or as they engage in a discussion. Varying the group size and group composition will provide students with many perspectives for consideration. For more information, see Center for Gifted Education (2011).

The models are listed below and described in the pages that follow.

1. Identity Chart
2. Literature Analysis Model
3. Primary Source Document Analysis Model
4. Music Analysis Model
5. Art Analysis Model

Identity Chart

The Identity Chart (see Figure 2) allows students to consider the concept of identity as they study the events of the late-20th century and examine the effect of those events on the American identity. Some scholars (Huntington, 2004; Smith, 2010) have defined the elements that comprise identity; for purposes of this unit, these include:

- » time and place,
- » history and myths,
- » culture and traditions,
- » race and ethnicity,
- » civic identity,
- » international role, and
- » economy.

Prior to the first lesson, you may have students develop a list of the elements that they believe are part of the American identity, and then compare it to the one listed here. Have students determine the definition of each element and give examples.

Tell students that in this unit, they will be examining the American identity in the 1980s, trying to get a better understanding of why Americans interacted as they did. Explain that identity is important because it shapes our actions and interactions with others. Have students answer the following questions on their own, then debrief in the large group:

- » Do all of the elements of identity that we listed affect your actions equally at all times? Explain your answer.
- » Sometimes various elements of identity are emphasized more than others. What are some examples? Why does this happen?
- » When is each of these elements most important? Least important? Why?
- » Which elements are most influential on your actions when you are at school? When you go on vacation? When you meet someone new? When you have to make an important decision? Why?

Explain that the questions and responses just discussed address individual (personal) identity. Have students answer the following questions:

- » What other types of identity are there?
- » How can a group's identity be different from an individual's identity within that group?

HANDOUT

Identity Chart

Identity	Time and Place
	Culture and Traditions
	History and Myths
	International Role
	Economy
	Civic Identity
	Race/Ethnicity

Figure 2. Identity Chart.

This discussion serves as the initial one regarding identity, specifically the American identity in the 1980s. Other unit activities will reinforce this concept. Teachers should revisit the identity generalizations regularly throughout the unit and make specific connections to the 1980s.

Literature Analysis Model

The Literature Analysis Model (see Figure 3) encourages students to consider seven aspects of a selection they are reading: key words, tone, mood, imagery, symbolism, key ideas, and the structure of writing (Center for Gifted Education, 2011; McKeague, 2009; National Governors Association Center for Best Practices & Council of Chief State School Officers, 2010). After reading a selection, this model helps students to organize their initial responses and provides them with a basis for discussing the piece in small or large groups. Whenever possible, students should be allowed to underline and make notes as they read the material. After marking the text, they can organize their notes into the model.

HANDOUT

Literature Analysis Model

Chosen or assigned text: _____
Key words:
Important ideas:
Tone:
Mood:
Imagery:
Symbolism:
Structure of writing:

Figure 3. Literature Analysis Model.

Suggested questions for completing and discussing the model are:

1. **Key words:** What words are important for understanding the selection? Which words did the author use for emphasis?
2. **Important ideas:** What is the main idea of the selection? What are other important ideas in the selection?
3. **Tone:** What is the attitude or what are the feelings of the author toward the subject of the selection? What words does the author use to indicate tone?
4. **Mood:** What emotions do you feel when reading the selection? How do the setting, images, objects, and details contribute to the mood?
5. **Imagery:** What are examples of the descriptive language that is used to create sensory impressions in the selection?
6. **Symbolism:** What symbols are used to represent other things?
7. **Structure of writing:** What are some important characteristics of the way this piece is written? How do the parts of this selection fit together and relate to each other? How do structural elements contribute to the meaning of the piece?

After students have completed their Literature Analysis Models individually, they should compare their answers in small groups. These small groups may compile a composite model that includes the ideas of all members. Following the small-group work, teachers have several options for using the models. For instance, they may ask each group to report to the class, they may ask groups to post their composite models, or they may develop a new Literature Analysis Model with the class based on the small-group work. It is important for teachers to hold a whole-group discussion as the final aspect of implementing this model as a teaching-learning device. Teachers are also encouraged to display the selection on a document camera or overhead projector as it is discussed and make appropriate annotations. The teacher should record ideas, underline words listed, and call attention to student responses visually. The teacher should conclude the discussion by asking open-ended follow-up questions. For more information about analyzing literature, see Center for Gifted Education (2011).

Primary Source Document Analysis Model

The Primary Source Document Analysis Model has been developed as a way to teach students:

- » how to interpret a historical document,
- » how to pose questions to ask about it, and
- » how to examine information in the document critically.

The handout (see Figure 4) is designed to assist students as they work through this Primary Source Document Analysis Model. The information that follows includes additional questions and ideas meant to facilitate use of the model. This questions in this model assume the author had an agenda or plan about a specific issue. Thus, it may not be appropriate for use with all primary source documents. For more information about primary sources, see Center for Gifted Education (2007) and Library of Congress (n.d.).

What is the title of the document? Why was it given this title? Students should write the title of the document in this space. The discussion should include probing of why the document was given this title.

What is your reaction to the document? The student will engage with the document and use prior knowledge to make some initial observations and comments. To do that, have students read the document and answer the questions based on their first impressions. You could also revisit the questions on this part of the model after a more thorough analysis of the document has been completed.

When was the document written? Why was it written? The student will focus on the context of the document, as well as its purpose. In order to do that, students must consider the following:

1. Students need to understand the beliefs, norms, and values—the *culture*—of the period in which the document was developed.
2. Students also need to think about other *relevant events* and prevalent opinions concerning this issue that were occurring at the time the document was created.
3. Students need to consider the *context*. Additional questions to explore the context could include:

HANDOUT

Primary Source Document Analysis Model

Document: _____

What is the title of the document? Why was it given this title?

Title:
Why do you think it was given this title?
Which words in the title are especially important? Why?

What is your reaction to the document?

What is the first thing about this document that draws your attention?
What is in the document that surprises you, or that you didn't expect?
What are some of the powerful ideas expressed in the document?
What feelings does the primary source cause in you?
What questions does it raise for you?

When was the document written? Why was it written?

Who is the author(s)?
When was the document written?
What do you know about the culture of the time period in which the document was written?
What were the important events occurring at the time the document was written?
What was the author's purpose in writing this document?
Who is the intended audience?
What biases do you see in the author's text?

What are the important ideas in this document?

What problems or events does the document address?
What is the author's main point or argument?
What actions or outcomes does the author expect? From whom?
How do you think this author would define _American identity_? What elements of the American identity does the author see as being threatened or cultivated? Why?

What is your evaluation of this document?

Is this document authentic? How do you know?
Is this author a reliable source for addressing this issue/problem?
How representative is this document of the views of the people at this time in history?
How does this document compare with others of the same time period?
What could have been the possible consequences of this document?
What actually happened as a result of this document? Discuss the long-term, short-term, and unintended consequences.
What interpretation of this historical period does this document provide?
How does this document contribute to your understanding of the American identity during this time period?

Figure 4. Primary Source Document Analysis Model.

- ○ Who had control of the situation? Who wanted control, but didn't have it?
- ○ Who and what were important to people at this time?
- ○ What did people at this time hope for or value?
- ○ Was this issue a new one, an ongoing one, one that was being debated frequently at the time, or one in which few people were interested?
- ○ What were the major events occurring at the time this document was written?
- ○ What were the societal trends occurring at the time this document was written?

4. Once students have determined the context for the document, the next step is to focus on the *purpose* of the document. Additional questions to explore the purpose include:
   - ○ Why did the author write this?
   - ○ Did a specific event or opinion of the time inspire this document? If so, what was it?
   - ○ Did the author have a personal experience that led him or her to write this?
   - ○ Did someone require or ask the author to write the document?
   - ○ How does the purpose affect the content of the document?

5. Connected to purpose is the *audience*. The same author may write differently for specific groups of people. The primary audience can affect the interpretation of the document.
   - ○ For whom was the document created?
   - ○ How did the proposed audience affect the content of the document?

What are the important ideas in this document? Once students understand the context and purpose of the document, they will analyze what the document means. Additional questions for probing student understanding of the document's *important ideas* could include:

- » What assumptions/values/feelings are reflected in the document?
- » What is the author's opinion about the issue?
- » Is the author empathetic about the situation, or critical of it?
- » Is the author an insider or outsider relative to the issue? Is the author personally involved with the issue or is he or she an observer?

Finally, because the author had a purpose for writing the document, he or she must expect something to happen as a result. These questions can provide additional prompting of student understanding of the *possible results*:

- » Who does the author expect to take action in this situation?
- » Does the author expect people to change their opinions, to take a specific action, or to consider a new idea?

What is your evaluation of this document? Students will evaluate the document to identify its effectiveness, both for those in the past and for us in the present.

1. The first set of questions focuses on the *authenticity* and *reliability* of a source to help students decide whether or not a document is what it claims or appears to be.
   - ○ Authenticity relates to whether the document is real, and not altered or an imitation. Historical documents often have passed through many hands; in doing so, editors or translators may have altered the words or the meaning of the document accidentally or intentionally to reflect their own agendas (Center for Gifted Education, 2007).

○ Reliability relates to the author's qualifications for addressing a given issue or event. In order to write something reliable, authors need to have adequate information and experience with the topic being discussed (Center for Gifted Education, 2007).

Additional questions for discussing the authenticity and reliability of a source are:
» Could the document have been fabricated, edited, or mistranslated?
» What evidence do you need to verify the accuracy of the document?
» What evidence do you have to show that the document was altered at a later time?
» How reliable is this author?
» Is the author an authority on this issue, or does he or she have sufficient knowledge to write about it?

2. The second set of questions focuses on how *representative* a document is of views of the time. This requires students to identify the prevalence of the stated ideas in society at the time the document was written.
   ○ Would many, some, or few people have agreed with the ideas stated in this document?
   ○ How do the ideas in this document relate to the context of the period in which it was written?
   ○ How does this document compare with others from the same period? Are there other documents from the time that express similar ideas? Different ideas?
   ○ What other information might you need to confirm this?

3. The third set of questions relates to considering the *consequences* of a document. First, students must consider the possible outcomes and then the actual ones. By considering the possible outcomes, students can see that multiple options for outcomes existed.
   ○ What could the possible consequences of this document have been?
   ○ What might happen if the author's plans were implemented?
   ○ What could the reaction to the author be when people read this?
   ○ How might this document affect or change public opinions?
   ○ What actually happened as a result of this document?
   ○ How did this document affect people's lives or events at the time (short-term effects)?
   ○ How did the document affect people at other times in the past, or how does it affect us today (long-term effects)?
   ○ What were the unintended consequences of this document?

4. The fourth set of questions helps students to determine *how the interpretation informs* the reader about the historical period:
   ○ What new interpretation of the historical period does this document provide for the reader?
   ○ How does the document provide an interpretation about the historical period that is not provided through other materials of the time?
   ○ How does this interpretation inform us about the American identity during this time period?

The implementation of this model may be handled similarly to the way in which discussions are held using the Literature Analysis Model: After students have completed their Primary Source Document Analysis Models individually, they should compare their answers in small groups. These small groups may compile a composite model that includes the ideas of all of the members. Following the small-group work, teachers have several options for using the models, including developing a composite, whole-class model, or posting group models and discussing them. It is important for teachers to hold a group discussion as the final aspect of implementing this model as a teaching-learning device. Teachers are also encouraged to display the selection on a document camera or overhead projector as it is discussed and make appropriate annotations. The teacher should record ideas, underline words listed, and call attention to student responses visually. The teacher should conclude the discussion by asking open-ended follow-up questions.

Music Analysis Model

The Music Analysis Model (see Figure 5) has been developed as a means for teaching students:
- » how to interpret lyrics from a song,
- » how to pose questions to ask about it, and
- » how to examine information in the song critically.

When working with specific songs, encourage students to think critically about both the *lyrics* and *orchestration*, keeping the elements of identity in mind. The Music Analysis Model uses the same key questions as the Primary Source Document Analysis Model, but with wording specifically related to songs:
- » What is the title of the song? Why was it given this title?
- » What is your reaction to the song?
- » When was the song written? Why was it written?
- » What are the important ideas in this song?
- » What is your evaluation of this song?

As such, many of the same questions listed above for the Primary Source Document Analysis Model may be used for additional probing into student understanding. For additional suggestions about the implementation of this model, please see the note regarding how to manage class discussions after students have completed the Primary Source Document Analysis Model.

Art Analysis Model

The Art Analysis Model (see Figure 6) has been developed as a means for teaching students:
- » how to interpret a piece of artwork,
- » how to pose questions to ask about it, and
- » how to examine the piece of artwork critically.

HANDOUT

Music Analysis Model

Song Title:_____

What is the title of the song? Why was it given this title?

Title:
Why do you think it was given this title?
Which words in the title are especially important? Why?

What is your reaction to the song?

What is the first thing about this song that draws your attention?
What is in the song that surprises you, or that you didn't expect?
What are some of the powerful ideas expressed in the song?
What feelings does the song cause in you?
What questions does it raise for you?

When was the song written? Why was it written?

Who is the songwriter(s)?
When was the song written?
What is the song's purpose? To entertain? To dance to? To critique something?
What were the important events occurring at the time the song was written?
Who is the intended audience?
What biases do you see in the author's lyrics?

What are the important ideas in this song?

Lyrics	Music/Accompaniment
What is the subject of the song? Summarize the song.	Describe the music or melody of this song. Is it fast-paced or slow? Does it have low notes or high notes? Is it melodic or does it have lots of percussion?
What are the main points of the song? What is the song saying about the subject?	What feelings do you get from the music? Why?
What mood/values/feelings does the singer have about the topic?	How does the tone or mood of the music fit with the lyrics? Why might this be?

What is your evaluation of this song?

What new or different interpretation of this historical period does this song provide?
What does this song portray about American identity or how Americans felt at the time?

Figure 5. Music Analysis Model.

HANDOUT

Art Analysis Model

Artist: _____

Artwork/Image: _____

What is the title of the artwork? Why was it given this title?

Title:
Why do you think it was given this title?
Which words in the title are especially important? Why?
What does the title reveal about the artwork?

What do you see in the artwork?

What objects, shapes, or people do you see?
What colors does the artist use? Why?
Are the images in the work realistic or abstract?
What materials does the artist use? Why?

What is your reaction to the image?

What is the first thing about this image that draws your attention?
What is in the image that surprises you, or that you didn't expect?
What are some of the powerful ideas expressed in the image?
What feelings does the image cause in you?
What questions does it raise for you?

When was the image produced? Why was it produced?

Who is the artist?
When was the artwork produced?
What were the important events occurring at the time the artwork was produced?
What was the author's purpose in producing this artwork?
Who is the intended audience?

What are the important ideas in this artwork?

What assumptions/values/feelings are reflected in the artwork?
What are the artist's views about the issue(s)?

What is your evaluation of this artwork?

What new or different interpretation of this historical period does this artwork provide?
What does this artwork portray about American identity or how Americans felt at the time?

Figure 6. Art Analysis Model.

When working with specific pieces of art, encourage students to think critically about both the *image* and the *materials*, keeping the elements of identity in mind. The Art Analysis Model uses many of the same key questions as the Primary Source Document Analysis Model, but with wording specifically related to artwork:

» What is the title of the artwork? Why was it given this title?
» What do you see in the artwork?
» What is your reaction to the image?
» When was the image produced? Why was it produced?
» What are the important ideas in this artwork?
» What is your evaluation of this artwork?

For additional suggestions about the implementation of this model, please see the note regarding how to manage class discussions after students have completed the Primary Source Document Analysis Model.

Summary: Teaching Models

The five teaching models that are included in this unit are essential for facilitating discussions and attaining unit objectives. Teachers should familiarize themselves with these models before beginning the unit and attempt to use them with fidelity. It is important that they use the models repeatedly, as students need practice interacting with the models' components and understanding the questions.

LESSON 1
The Inauguration of Ronald Reagan

Alignment of Unit Goals

- » Goal 1: To understand the concept of identity in 1980s America.
- » Goal 2: To develop skills in historical analysis and song and artwork interpretation.
- » Goal 3: To develop analytical and interpretive skills in literature.
- » Goal 4: To develop an understanding of historical events occurring in the United States during the 1980s.

Unit Objectives

- » To describe how the American identity changed during the 1980s.
- » To describe how changes in American identity in the 1980s were revealed in the music, art, and literature of the decade.

» To define the context in which a song or piece of art was produced and the implications of context for understanding the artifact.

» To describe a writer's or artist's intent in producing a given song or piece of art based on understanding of text and context.

» To describe what a selected literary passage means.

» To describe major historical events during the 1980s that affected the American identity.

» To describe music, art, and literature of the 1980s that reflected the American identity.

Resources for Unit Implementation

» **Handout 1.1:** Music Analysis Model

» **Handout 1.2:** The Early 1980s

» **Handout 1.3:** Identity Chart

» **Handout 1.4:** Music Analysis Model

» **Handout 1.5:** Art Analysis Model

» **Handout 1.6:** Identity Generalizations

» **Handout 1.7:** Unit Project: All I Really Needed to Know I Learned in the 1980s

» **Listen:** "Girls Just Want to Have Fun" (Hazard, 1983) by Cyndi Lauper; "I Wanna Dance with Somebody (Who Loves Me)" (Merrill & Rubicam, 1987) by Whitney Houston; "Walking on Sunshine" (Rew, 1983) by Katrina and the Waves; and "Everybody Have Fun Tonight" (Hues, Feldman, & Wolf, 1986) by Wang Chung. All of the songs are available on YouTube.

» **Read:** Ronald Reagan's first inaugural address, available at: http://www.bartleby.com/124/pres61.html

» **Watch:** Music videos for "Girls Just Want to Have Fun" (Hazard, 1983) by Cyndi Lauper and "I Wanna Dance with Somebody (Who Loves Me)" (Merrill & Rubican, 1987) by Whitney Houston. Both music videos are available on YouTube.

» **Listen:** "God Bless the USA" by Lee Greenwood (1984) and "In America" (Daniels, Crain, DiGregorio, Edwards, Marshall, & Hayward, 1980) by The Charlie Daniels Band. Both songs are available on YouTube.

» **View/Read:** Artwork by and information Keith Haring, available at http://www.haring.com/!/about-haring#.U3JPJK1dXWE and http://www.haring.com/!/introduction#.U3JPfK1dXWE

Key Terms

» *Assassination:* the murder of a political figure, often by a surprise attack

» *Inauguration:* the official and ceremonial induction of a person into a government office

» *Omnibus:* including or relating to many items

Learning Experiences

1. Review with students the events of the 1970s that they have learned thus far. **Ask:** What events do you remember from the 1970s? What were some major political events? What

was going on in the United States economically? Who were the presidents from 1970 to 1980? What was the mood of the American people by the end of the 1970s?

2. Give students Handout 1.1 (Music Analysis Sheet) and play the songs of the early 1980s: "Girls Just Want to Have Fun" (Hazard, 1983) by Cyndi Lauper; "I Wanna Dance with Somebody (Who Loves Me)" (Merrill & Rubicam, 1987) by Whitney Houston; "Walking on Sunshine" (Rew, 1983) by Katrina and the Waves; and "Everybody Have Fun Tonight" (Feldman, Hues, & Wolf, 1986) by Wang Chung. Have students do a composite analysis of the songs. Have students watch the music videos for the Cyndi Lauper and Whitney Houston songs; both videos give a light-hearted energy to the songs. **Ask:** What is the mood of these songs? Why might this be? Think about the music of the late 1970s we just studied, how are these similar? Different? Why might that be?

3. Explain that in the fall of 1980, Americans elected a new president, Ronald Reagan, and in January 1981, he gave his first inaugural address. Have students read Reagan's first inaugural address and use Handout 1.2 (The Early 1980s) to analyze the speech. **Ask:** How did Ronald Reagan view America and Americans? What traits or characteristics did he identify? What was his mood in this speech? How did he view the future? How do you think Americans felt about this speech given the events of the last decade?

4. Distribute Handout 1.3 (Identity Chart) to students and explain that some scholars have developed categories of elements that define identity such as family, race, ethnicity, individuality, beliefs, values, nationality, social class, time, and place. Have them use these and other elements to try to define American identity in the 1980s. Tell students they are going to use this chart to analyze President Reagan's speech and what it says about American identity in 1980. **Ask:**
   a. Time and place: What was our nationality? What were our national symbols and sources of pride? What shared symbols or traditions represented American identity and were seen as meaningful by most Americans?
   b. History and myths: What elements of the shared background or heritage of the U.S. did Ronald Reagan mention? What recent events or experiences shaped American views?
   c. Culture and traditions: What traits did Ronald Reagan stress about Americans?
   d. Race and ethnicity: What was the status of the races in 1980? What did President Reagan say about racial differences?
   e. Civic identity: What was the role of the citizen in America? What were our rights and duties as citizens in Reagan's speech?
   f. International role: What beliefs did President Reagan have about America? How did he view other countries?
   g. Economy: What were the major goods and services that the U.S. produced? How did the U.S. generate revenue? What types of jobs did most people have? What was the status of the U.S. economy?

5. Explain to students that immediately after President Reagan was inaugurated, the hostages in Iran were freed without our government doing anything. In March of 1981, there was an assassination attempt on President Reagan that he survived; he was soon making jokes from his recovery room, which increased American support of him. In 1981, President Reagan passed a massive tax cut, the Economic Recovery Tax Act, followed

by the Omnibus Budget Reconciliation Act in 1983, which cut government spending. Reagan also took a decisive stance in the Air Traffic Controller Strike of 1981 by ordering the strikers back to work and firing the ones who didn't comply. By 1983, the economy was starting to improve and these events changed the mood of the country. Have students listen to and analyze Lee Greenwood's (1984) "God Bless the USA" and The Charlie Daniels Band's "In America" (Daniels, Crain, DiGregorio, Edwards, Marshall, & Hayward, 1980). Have students complete Handout 1.4 (Music Analysis Model). **Ask:** How do these two songs view the U.S.? What is the mood of these two songs? How are the mood and idea of these songs similar to what President Reagan said in his inauguration speech? How are they different? What does this tell you about Americans in the 1980s?

6. Tell students that one artist who captured the energy and spirit of the 1980s was Keith Haring. Give students Handout 1.5 (Art Analysis Model). Have students analyze the images of Keith Haring's art and read the text using the webpages listed under "Resources for Unit Implementation." **Ask:** What colors did Keith Haring use? What is the mood of his art? How does it make you feel? What does this art reveal about the 1980s?

7. Explain to students that they will look at how these forces and others altered American identity using a set of generalizations. Distribute Handout 1.6 (Identity Generalizations) to students and explain that they will work through it by responding to related questions.

    a. The first generalization is *"Identity changes with new ideas, experiences, conditions, or in response to other expressions of identity."* **Ask:** What new ideas, experiences, or conditions arose during the late 1970s and early 1980s? How did these ideas, experiences, or conditions affect American identity?

    b. The second generalization is *"Identity is created by a group, person, or outsiders, and self-created identities may be different from how others see one's self."* **Ask:** How did America see itself in the world? How did the Soviet Union see America? How did the U.S. see the Soviet Union and Latin America? How did these different views shape America's role in the world?

    c. The third generalization is *"There are multiple elements of identity and at different times, different elements have greater or lesser importance."* **Ask:** Which elements of identity were most significant in 1980? How did this change from what they were in 1970?

    d. The fourth generalization is *"Although members of a group or society may have different individual identities, they still share particular elements of identity."* **Ask:** Despite individual differences, which elements of identity did all Americans have in common?

8. Explain the unit project to students and distribute Handout 1.7 (Unit Project: All I Really Needed to Know I Learned in the 1980s). Tell students that this will be a way for them to pull together and summarize the entire decade. Go over the project with students and tell them to write down ideas as they work through the unit.

Assessing Student Learning

» Handout 1.1 (Music Analysis Model)
» Handout 1.2 (The Early 1980s)
» Handout 1.3 (Identity Chart)

» Handout 1.4 (Music Analysis Model)
» Handout 1.5 (Art Analysis Model)
» Handout 1.6 (Identity Generalizations)
» Discussions

Extending Student Learning

The following are optional activities for extending student learning in this lesson:

» As an independent or group research activity, have students analyze Reagan's first inaugural address. Have them review the address and discuss (in oral or written form) the state of the country at the time the inaugural address was given, the major ideas presented, the goals proposed by the president, whether the stated goals were attained, famous quotations from the speech, and reactions to the address.

» Have students research "Reaganomics," the economic policies promoted by Ronald Reagan while he was president. Students should discuss what the term means, the key components of the policies, and how/whether the policies are still in effect today. Have students present the information in an interactive format.

HANDOUT 1.1
Music Analysis Model

Directions: After listening to "Girls Just Want to Have Fun," "I Wanna Dance with Somebody," "Walking on Sunshine," and "Everybody Have Fun Tonight," please complete the following questions.

Song Title:_____

What is the title of the song? Why was it given this title?

Title:
Why do you think it was given this title?
Which words in the title are especially important? Why?

What is your reaction to the song?

What is the first thing about this song that draws your attention?
What is in the song that surprises you, or that you didn't expect?
What are some of the powerful ideas expressed in the song?
What feelings does the song cause in you?
What questions does it raise for you?

Name: _____ Date: _____

When was the song written? Why was it written?

Who is the songwriter(s)?	
When was the song written?	
What is the song's purpose? To entertain? To dance to? To critique something?	
What were the important events occurring at the time the song was written?	
Who is the intended audience?	
What biases do you see in the author's lyrics?	

What are the important ideas in this song?

Lyrics	Music/Accompaniment
What is the subject of the song? Summarize the song.	Describe the music or melody of this song. Is it fast-paced or slow? Does it have low notes or high notes? Is it melodic or does it have lots of percussion?
What are the main points of the song? What is the song saying about the subject?	What feelings do you get from the music? Why?
What mood/values/feelings does the singer have about the topic?	How does the tone or mood of the music fit with the lyrics? Why might this be?

What is your evaluation of this song?

What new or different interpretation of this historical period does this song provide?	
What does this song portray about American identity or how Americans felt at the time?	

HANDOUT 1.2
The Early 1980s

Directions: After reading Reagan's first inaugural address, answer the following questions.

1. What problems does he identify in the United States?

2. What solutions or promises does he present or make?

3. How does he view America and Americans? What traits or characteristics does he identify?

4. What is his mood in this speech? How does he view the future?

5. What historical references does he make? Why does he choose these stories and examples? What point is he making?

6. How might Americans feel about this speech given the events of the last decade?

Name:_____ Date:_____

HANDOUT 1.3

Identity Chart

Directions: Complete each box with the elements that define each category of identity.

Identity	Time and Place
	Culture and Traditions
	History and Myths
	International Role
	Economy
	Civic Identity
	Race/Ethnicity

Name: _____ Date: _____

HANDOUT 1.4
Music Analysis Model

Directions: After listening to "God Bless the USA" by Lee Greenwood or "In America" by the Charlie Daniels Band, please complete these questions.

Song Title: _____

What is the title of the song? Why was it given this title?

Title:
Why do you think it was given this title?
Which words in the title are especially important? Why?

What is your reaction to the song?

What is the first thing about this song that draws your attention?
What is in the song that surprises you, or that you didn't expect?
What are some of the powerful ideas expressed in the song?
What feelings does the song cause in you?
What questions does it raise for you?

Name:_____ Date:_____

When was the song written? Why was it written?

Who is the songwriter(s)?
When was the song written?
What is the song's purpose? To entertain? To dance to? To critique something?
What were the important events occurring at the time the song was written?
Who is the intended audience?
What biases do you see in the author's lyrics?

What are the important ideas in this song?

Lyrics	Music/Accompaniment
What is the subject of the song? Summarize the song.	Describe the music or melody of this song. Is it fast-paced or slow? Does it have low notes or high notes? Is it melodic or does it have lots of percussion?
What are the main points of the song? What is the song saying about the subject?	What feelings do you get from the music? Why?
What mood/values/feelings does the singer have about the topic?	How does the tone or mood of the music fit with the lyrics? Why might this be?

What is your evaluation of this song?

What new or different interpretation of this historical period does this song provide?
What does this song portray about American identity or how Americans felt at the time?

HANDOUT 1.5

Art Analysis Model

Directions: Complete these questions after reviewing the art of Keith Haring.

Artist: _____

Artwork/Image: _____

What is the title of the artwork? Why was it given this title?

Title:
Why do you think it was given this title?
Which words in the title are especially important? Why?
What does the title reveal about the artwork?

What do you see in the artwork?

What objects, shapes, or people do you see?
What colors does the artist use? Why?
Are the images in the work realistic or abstract?
What materials does the artist use? Why?

What is your reaction to the image?

What is the first thing about this image that draws your attention?

Handout 1.5: Art Analysis Model, continued

What is in the image that surprises you, or that you didn't expect?
What are some of the powerful ideas expressed in the image?
What feelings does the image cause in you?
What questions does it raise for you?

When was the image produced? Why was it produced?

Who is the artist?
When was the artwork produced?
What were the important events occurring at the time the artwork was produced?
What was the author's purpose in producing this artwork?
Who is the intended audience?

What are the important ideas in this artwork?

What assumptions/values/feelings are reflected in the artwork?
What are the artist's views about the issue(s)?

What is your evaluation of this artwork?

What new or different interpretation of this historical period does this artwork provide?
What does this artwork portray about American identity or how Americans felt at the time?

HANDOUT 1.6

Identity Generalizations

Directions: Use these generalizations to frame your discussion of how the events and experiences of the 1980s altered the American identity.

Identity changes with new ideas, experiences, conditions, or in response to other expressions of identity.
Identity is created by a group, person, or outsiders, and self-created identities may be different from how others see one's self.
There are multiple elements of identity and at different times, different elements have greater or lesser importance.
Although members of a group or society may have different individual identities, they still share particular elements of identity.

HANDOUT 1.7

Unit Project:
All I Really Need to Know
I Learned From the 1980s

In 1989, Robert Fulghum published a book entitled *All I Really Need to Know I Learned in Kindergarten*, which was a series of essays. The title piece was eventually made into posters, greeting cards, and often posted as an inspirational message. Because one goal of studying history is to learn from the past and use that knowledge to move forward to a better future, you are going to think about what lessons Americans today can take from the 1980s.

The text of the title essay, "All I Really Need to Know I Learned in Kindergarten," can be found at http://scrapbook.com/poems/doc/842.html.

Your task: Based on your understanding of the 1980s, create your own poem about what Americans should learn from the events and experiences of this decade. The original text is several short sentences of what Fulghum learned and read as a list. Your piece will start with the same three lines as Fulghum's and an altered fourth line:

"Most of what I really need
To know about how to live
And what to do and how to be
I learned from studying the 1980s"

Based on what you have studied and learned from the 1980s you need to add:

» a minimum of 10 statements of things Americans can learn from what happened in the 1980s;
» mistakes or bad things that happened in the 1980s and what we can learn about how to avoid repeating such things;
» the positive experiences of 1980s and what we did well in that decade;
» the missed opportunities of the 1980s and what citizens or politicians almost did but didn't achieve;
» a separate explanation of your lessons–for each of the statements you put in your poem, write an explanation of what event or person your lesson comes from and how you developed your statement from their actions; and
» prominent events or experiences from the decade; you are not restricted to the ones you listened to or read about in the unit.

This assignment will be due during Lesson 10, the last lesson of the unit.

LESSON 2

The Evil Empire: The Cold War Heats Up

Alignment of Unit Goals

- » Goal 1: To understand the concept of identity in 1980s America.
- » Goal 2: To develop skills in historical analysis and song and artwork interpretation.
- » Goal 3: To develop analytical and interpretive skills in literature.
- » Goal 4: To develop an understanding of historical events occurring in the United States during the 1980s.

Unit Objectives

- » To describe how the American identity changed during the 1980s.
- » To describe how changes in American identity in the 1980s were revealed in the music, art, and literature of the decade.

» To define the context in which a song or piece of art was produced and the implications of context for understanding the artifact.

» To describe a writer's or artist's intent in producing a given song or piece of art based on understanding of text and context.

» To describe what a selected literary passage means.

» To describe major historical events during the 1980s that affected the American identity.

» To describe music, art, and literature of the 1980s that reflected the American identity.

Resources for Unit Implementation

» **Handout 2.1:** Cold War Warriors

» **Handout 2.2:** Nuclear War Song Analysis

» **Read:** Information on Ronald Reagan's Strategic Defense Initiative, available at http://coldwar.org/articles/80s/SDI-StarWars.asp

» **Read:** Ronald Reagan's 1983 speech at the 41st Annual Convention of the National Association of Evangelicals: http://www.americanrhetoric.com/speeches/ronaldreagan evilempire.htm

» **Read:** Chapter 1 of Tom Clancy's (1984/2010) *The Hunt for Red October*, which can be found at http://www.tomclancy.com/excerpts/hunt_for_red_october_clancy.pdf

» **Listen:** "Ronnie, Talk to Russia" by Prince (1981); "99 Red Balloons" (McAlea, 1984) by Nena; "Fight Fire with Fire" (Hetfield, Burton, & Ulrich, 1984) by Metallica; "Burning Heart" (Peterik & Sullivan, 1985) by Survivor; and "Christmas at Ground Zero" by Weird Al Yankovic (1986). All of the songs are available on YouTube.

» **Watch:** Music video for "Christmas at Ground Zero" (Yankovic, 1986). Available on YouTube.

Key Terms

» *Cold War:* The Cold War was a lengthy state of military and political tension between countries in the Western Bloc (the United States with NATO and others) and powers in the Eastern Bloc (the Soviet Union and its allies of the Warsaw Pact).

Learning Experiences

1. Have students use their textbooks to review events of the 1970s. **Ask:** What was the Cold War? What interactions and tensions did we see between the United States and the Soviet Union during the 1950s? In the 1960s? In the 1970s? What was the détente? How had relationships with the Soviets changed since the end of World War II? What was the trend by the end of the 1970s? What events and countries had really been our focus in the 1970s?

2. Explain that when Ronald Reagan became president, he wanted to increase our defenses against the Soviet Union. Go over his Strategic Defense Initiative (sometimes nicknamed "Star Wars") with students. President Reagan expressed his stance in a speech he gave to a meeting of the National Association of Evangelists on March 8, 1983. Give students

Handout 2.1 (Cold War Warriors) and copy of Reagan's speech to analyze. (The URL to the speech is listed under "Resources for Unit Implementation.") Discuss student responses. **Ask:** How did President Reagan describe the Soviets? What did he ask of Americans? Why? How did he view the world and the Cold War? How are these views different from what we saw in the 1970s? Why? Given the events of the past decade, how do you think Americans responded to President Reagan's speech? Why would Americans support President Reagan's position? What do you think critics said about his speech?

3. Explain to students that after this speech, in 1984, Tom Clancy wrote his first published novel, *The Hunt for Red October*, about a CIA agent, Jack Ryan, and the Soviet Union. The book was made into a Hollywood film. Have students read the first chapter of the book and answer the questions on Handout 2.1 (Cold War Warriors). Discuss student responses. **Ask:** What was Clancy's view of the Soviets and the Cold War? What was his mood concerning world events and the U.S.'s position in them? The story is about Soviet military personnel trying to escape and defect to the United States; what does that tell us about how Clancy viewed the U.S. and the Soviet Union? Do you think Americans agreed with his view? Why might his book be appealing to Americans?

4. Americans listened to songs about nuclear war and the Soviet Union in previous decades. **Ask:** What has been the mood of those songs? What do you expect to see in the 1980s based on what you have read? Give students Handout 2.2 (Nuclear War Song Analysis). Have students listen to "Ronnie, Talk to Russia" by Prince (1981); "99 Red Balloons" (McAlea, 1984) by Nena; "Fight Fire with Fire" (Hetfield, Burton, & Ulrich, 1984) by Metallica; "Burning Heart" (Peterik & Sullivan, 1985) by Survivor; and "Christmas at Ground Zero" by Weird Al Yankovic (1986). **Ask:** How do the moods of the songs match that of President Reagan's speech? How do they fit the mood of *The Hunt for Red October*? Why might this be? What does this tell us about the American people and their views of the Soviet Union and Cold War in the 1980s?

5. Have students use what they have learned to complete the identity chart on Handout 2.1 (Cold War Warriors). Discuss student responses. **Ask:** What events led to this new view of the Cold War and the Soviets? Why did we see an end to the détente of the 1970s and this increased tension? What identity did we create of the Soviets? Of ourselves? How did these views shape how we viewed and interacted with the Soviet Union? What were the advantages and the disadvantages of our changing views of the Soviets?

Assessing Student Learning

» Handout 2.1 (Cold War Warriors)
» Handout 2.2 (Nuclear War Song Analysis)
» Discussions

Extending Student Learning

The following are optional activities for extending student learning in this lesson:
» As an independent or group research activity, have students find information about some of the historic agreements that were made after World War II regarding the fate

of Germany and Eastern Europe. Have them research the Yalta Conference and the Potsdam Conference, then make a comprehensive list of agreements made at those events. Students should compare and contrast the agreements made at Yalta with those reached at Potsdam.

» Have students trace the history of the Cold War from its beginning to its end. Have them present the timeline using multimedia.

HANDOUT 2.1

Cold War Warriors

Directions: Respond to the following questions related to various components of this lesson.

President Reagan, Speech of March 8, 1983

1. How does Reagan feel about the proposed missile limitation agreement?

   _____

   _____

2. Why is he less willing to make agreements than Nixon and Carter had been?

   _____

   _____

3. How does he describe the Soviets?

   _____

   _____

4. What does he ask of Americans? Why?

   _____

   _____

5. How does he view the world and the Cold War?

   _____

   _____

6. How are these views different from what we saw in the 1970s? Why?

   _____

   _____

7. If the U.S. follows through on Reagan's ideas, what are the possible outcomes?

   _____

   _____

8. Given the events of the time, how do you think most Americans felt about Reagan's speech? Why?

   _____

   _____

Tom Clancy, *The Hunt for Red October*

1. What images of life in the Soviet Union do you get in this passage? How does he depict daily life?

   _____

   _____

2. What is Rodina? What is its role in the lives of a Soviet citizen? How do we see it in the excerpt?

   _____

   _____

3. What is the role of the political officer? What does it tell you about this society that they had to have a political officer?

   _____

   _____

4. How do the Russians in the excerpt talk about Americans? What does he mean by "imperialists"?

   _____

   _____

5. How are the Soviet views of themselves and us similar to Reagan's ideas? How are the Soviet views of the world and Cold War different?

   _____

   _____

6. What happens at the end of the chapter? What is the captain planning?

   _____

   _____

7. This book was written by an American. Do you think this book is realistic? What does this suggest about how Americans see themselves and the Cold War?

   _____

   _____

Handout 2.1: Cold War Warriors, continued

Identity Chart

After you have listened to the songs, complete the following:

Identity changes with new ideas, experiences, conditions, or in response to other expressions of identity.
What events led to this new view of the Cold War and the Soviets? Why did we see the end of the détente and this tension?
What were the effects on the U.S. of the Cold War intensifying? How did this affect us economically? Politically? Socially? How did it unite us? Divide us?
Identity is created by a group, person, or outsiders, and self-created identities may be different from how others see one's self.
What identity did we create of the Soviets? Of ourselves? How accurate were they? What was the effect of this? How did these views shape how we view and interact with the Soviet Union? What were the positives and the drawbacks of these identities?

Name:_____ Date:_____

HANDOUT 2.2
Nuclear War Song Analysis

Directions: Analyze the following songs and answer the two questions at the end of the handout.

"Ronnie, Talk to Russia" by Prince

Lyrics	Music/Accompaniment
What is the subject of the song? Summarize the song.	Describe the music or melody of this song. Is it fast paced or slow? Does it have low notes or high notes? Is it melodic or does it have lots of percussion?
What are the main points of the song? What is the song saying about the subject?	
	What feelings do you get from the music? Why?
What mood/values/feelings does the singer have about the topic?	How does the tone or mood of the music fit with the lyrics? Why might this be?

"99 Red Balloons" by Nena

Lyrics	Music/Accompaniment
What is the subject of the song? Summarize the song.	Describe the music or melody of this song. Is it fast paced or slow? Does it have low notes or high notes? Is it melodic or does it have lots of percussion?
What are the main points of the song? What is the song saying about the subject?	
	What feelings do you get from the music? Why?
What mood/values/feelings does the singer have about the topic?	How does the tone or mood of the music fit with the lyrics? Why might this be?

Name:_____ Date:_____

"Fight Fire with Fire" by Metallica

Lyrics	Music/Accompaniment
What is the subject of the song? Summarize the song.	Describe the music or melody of this song. Is it fast paced or slow? Does it have low notes or high notes? Is it melodic or does it have lots of percussion?
What are the main points of the song? What is the song saying about the subject?	What feelings do you get from the music? Why?
What mood/values/feelings does the singer have about the topic?	How does the tone or mood of the music fit with the lyrics? Why might this be?

"Burning Heart" by Survivor

Lyrics	Music/Accompaniment
What is the subject of the song? Summarize the song.	Describe the music or melody of this song. Is it fast paced or slow? Does it have low notes or high notes? Is it melodic or does it have lots of percussion?
What are the main points of the song? What is the song saying about the subject?	What feelings do you get from the music? Why?
What mood/values/feelings does the singer have about the topic?	How does the tone or mood of the music fit with the lyrics? Why might this be?

"Christmas at Ground Zero" by Weird Al Yankovic

Lyrics	Music/Accompaniment
What is the subject of the song? Summarize the song.	Describe the music or melody of this song. Is it fast paced or slow? Does it have low notes or high notes? Is it melodic or does it have lots of percussion?
What are the main points of the song? What is the song saying about the subject?	What feelings do you get from the music? Why?
What mood/values/feelings does the singer have about the topic?	How does the tone or mood of the music fit with the lyrics? Why might this be?

What is the overall mood of these songs?

_____

_____

_____

_____

_____

What new understanding about American history do you get from these songs?

_____

_____

_____

_____

_____

_____

LESSON 3

Changing Technology in the 1980s

Alignment of Unit Goals

- » Goal 1: To understand the concept of identity in 1980s America.
- » Goal 2: To develop skills in historical analysis and song and artwork interpretation.
- » Goal 3: To develop analytical and interpretive skills in literature.
- » Goal 4: To develop an understanding of historical events occurring in the United States during the 1980s.

Unit Objectives

- » To describe how the American identity changed during the 1980s.
- » To describe how changes in American identity in the 1980s were revealed in the music, art, and literature of the decade.

» To define the context in which a song or piece of art was produced and the implications of context for understanding the artifact.

» To describe a writer's or artist's intent in producing a given song or piece of art based on understanding of text and context.

» To describe what a selected literary passage means.

» To describe major historical events during the 1980s that affected the American identity.

» To describe music, art, and literature of the 1980s that reflected the American identity.

Resources for Unit Implementation

» **Handout 3.1:** Your Leisure Time

» **Handout 3.2:** Technology in the 1980s

» **Handout 3.3:** Identity in the Computer Age

» **Listen:** "Channel Z" by The B-52's (1989); "Pac-Man Fever" by Buckner and Garcia (1982); "Video Killed the Radio Star" (Downes, Horn, & Woolley, 1979) by The Buggles; and "Mr. Roboto" (DeYoung, 1983) by Styx. All of the songs are available on YouTube.

» **Read:** "Cyberpunk" by Bruce Bethke (1983), available at http://www.infinityplus.co.uk/stories/cpunk.htm

Key Terms

» *Leisure:* time when you are not working; free or unoccupied time

» *Technology:* a machine or piece of equipment developed to solve problems or make a process more efficient

Learning Experiences

1. Prior to the lesson, ask students to interview their parents and grandparents. **Have students ask their parents and grandparents:** What kinds of things did you do in your spare time when you were a child? When you were in middle school or high school, what did you do after school? What did you do on the weekends? **Have students bring this information to class on the day of this lesson.**

2. Give students Handout 3.1 (Your Leisure Time). Have students answer the questions and then report their responses and collect the information on the board. **Ask:** What would you do in your free time if you did not have a computer, video games, or cable television? How would your life be different? What kind of things did you find out your parents and grandparents did? How would you feel if your free time looked like your parents' free time when they were kids? Your grandparents'? What has changed to make your leisure time different from theirs?

3. Explain that in this lesson, students are going to look at some of the changes that came about in the 1980s and how people felt about them. Tell students that in 1981, home computers, MTV, and CNN were all invented. Explain that home computers at that time did not have Internet or e-mail, but did have games. In addition, home video games such as Atari and Nintendo started to increase their variety of games and gained popular-

ity in the early 1980s, and cable TV channels that focused on specialty programs like news (e.g., CNN), sports (e.g., ESPN), or music (e.g., MTV) all appeared. **Ask:** How do you think computers, video games, and cable TV changed the U.S.? What were the economic effects? Social effects? Political effects? How were the changes positive? How were they negative? How do you think people felt about these changes?

4. Give students Handout 3.2 (Technology in the 1980s). Have students listen to "Channel Z" by the B-52's (1989); "Pac-Man Fever" by Buckner and Garcia (1981); "Video Killed the Radio Star" (Downes, Horne, & Woolley, 1979) by The Buggles; and "Mr. Roboto" (DeYoung, 1983) by Styx and complete the handout. Discuss student responses. **Ask:** Beyond the song, think about how these new technologies changed the U.S. What moods or views of technology do you get from the songs? Do the songwriters like the new technology or dislike it? What emotions do they have? Why?

5. Have students read "Cyberpunk" by Bruce Bethke (1983) and answer the questions on Handout 3.2. Discuss student responses. **Ask:** What do you notice about the language and word choice? What do you think the purpose of changing the names of things this way is? What does it suggest about what changes the author thinks the computer age will bring? How does this story seem to view the new technology? According to the story, what are the benefits of computers? What are the drawbacks? How is technology affecting relations between the generations in the story?

6. Make a list of pros and cons for the following questions on the board or on student paper: What was good about the development of cable TV, video games, and home computers? From our 21st-century perspective, how have these technologies changed life in America for the better? What problems or divisions have they created?

7. Have students think of a new technology that has been recently introduced. **Ask:** What are some fears people have of this technology? What hopes do people have for the technology? How are our reactions to this new technology similar to reactions to computers and the technologies of the 1980s? Why do we have such mixed reactions to new technology? What does this tell us about Americans and American values? Why do we have such a tension between progress and remaining technologically static? Have students complete Handout 3.3 (Identity in the Computer Age) and discuss student responses.

Assessing Student Learning

» Handout 3.1 (Your Leisure Time)
» Handout 3.2 (Technology in the 1980s)
» Handout 3.3 (Identity in the Computer Age)
» Discussions

Extending Student Learning

The following are optional activities for extending student learning in this lesson:

» Have students research the history of a common technology, such as the television, cellular telephone, or computer. Have them present the information in a timeline format.

» Have students investigate the future of a common technology, such as the television, cellular telephone, or computer. Have them share their findings in a multimedia presentation.

» Have students use cartoon clips from *The Jetsons*, which aired from 1962–1987, to compare ideas about what future technologies would be like with what they are actually like now.

HANDOUT 3.1
Your Leisure Time

Directions: Respond to these questions. Be prepared to share the answers with your classmates.

1. Approximately how many hours a day do you spend playing computer games or video games?

_____
_____
_____
_____

2. Approximately how much time per day do you spend on your cell phone?

_____
_____
_____
_____

3. Approximately how much time per day do you spend watching TV?

_____
_____
_____
_____

4. When you watch TV, how much of what you watch is on NBC, CBS, or ABC?

_____
_____
_____
_____

5. If you pay attention to the news, where do you get your news from?

_____
_____
_____
_____

6. What would you do with your free time if you did not have a cell phone, computer, or video games?

_____
_____
_____
_____

Name:_____ Date:_____

HANDOUT 3.2
Technology in the 1980s

Directions: Complete this chart after listening to the songs, and then answer the question on the next page about "Cyberpunk."

	"Channel Z" by B-52s	"Pac-Man Fever" by Buckner & Garcia	"Video Killed the Radio Star" by The Buggles	"Mr. Roboto" by Styx
What new development is this song about?				
What is the mood or tone of the song? How does the song seem to feel about the new technology? Why?				
In what ways is this technology a positive? What benefits does it provide?				
In what ways is the technology in this song problematic? What are the drawbacks of it?				

"Cyberpunk" by Bruce Bethke

1. What do you notice about the language and word choice? What is the purpose of changing names of things this way? What does it suggest about what changes the author thinks the computer age will bring?

    _____

    _____

    _____

    _____

2. Who are the "Olders"? How do Rayno, Lisa, Georgie, and Mikey view them? Why?

    _____

    _____

    _____

    _____

3. What are Rayno, Lisa, Georgie, and Mikey doing in the story? What does Mikey do to his dad? Why? What happens to Mikey?

    _____

    _____

    _____

    _____

4. How does this story seem to view the new technology? What are the benefits of computers? What are the drawbacks? How is technology affecting relations between the generations?

    _____

    _____

    _____

    _____

Name:_____ Date:_____

HANDOUT 3.3

Identity in the Computer Age

Directions: Complete these questions about new technologies.

Identity changes with new ideas, experiences, conditions, or in response to other expressions of identity.
How were these new technologies changing American identity? Think about how you spend your free time and how your parents and grandparents spent their free time: What new values and experiences do we have now? How does that change American society and in what ways? What changes can you see in your interviews and your own life?
There are multiple elements of identity and at different times, *different elements have greater or lesser importance.*
What elements of identity become more important as technology changes? Think about the story: What values, knowledge, and concerns become more important? What elements of identity might become less important as a result of this new technology?

Although members of a group or society may have different individual identities, they still share particular elements of identity.
How does new technology promote individual identities? Some have said that due to cable TV, Americans are not watching the same things, so we have less in common. Do you agree? Why or why not? In what ways can these new technologies give us more in common? How do the new technologies help to unify and unite us?

LESSON 4

It's a Material World: Yuppies and the Affluence of the 1980s

Alignment of Unit Goals

>> Goal 1: To understand the concept of identity in 1980s America.
>> Goal 2: To develop skills in historical analysis and song and artwork interpretation.
>> Goal 3: To develop analytical and interpretive skills in literature.
>> Goal 4: To develop an understanding of historical events occurring in the United States during the 1980s.

Unit Objectives

>> To describe how the American identity changed during the 1980s.
>> To describe how changes in American identity in the 1980s were revealed in the music, art, and literature of the decade.

» Define the context in which a song or piece of art was produced and the implications of context for understanding the artifact.

» Describe a writer's or artist's intent in producing a given song or piece of art based on understanding of text and context.

» Describe what a selected literary passage means.

» Describe major historical events during the 1980s that affected the American identity.

» Describe music, art, and literature of the 1980s that reflected the American identity.

Resources for Unit Implementation

» **Handout 4.1:** The Material World

» **Handout 4.2:** Yuppies

» **Handout 4.3:** Beneath the Surface

» **Handout 4.4:** From Ideals to Critiques

» **Read:** "The Reagan Boom" by Martin Anderson (1990), available at http://www.nytimes.com/1990/01/17/opinion/the-reagan-boom-greatest-ever.html

» **Read:** Chapter 3 from *The Bonfire of the Vanities* by Tom Wolfe (1987/2008), available at http://www.tomwolfe.com/BonfireExcerpt.html

» **Listen:** "Material Girl" (Brown & Rans, 1984) by Madonna; and "Opportunities (Let's Make Lots of Money)" (Tennant & Lowe, 1984) by Pet Shop Boys. Both songs are available on YouTube.

» **View:** Images and clips from the television shows *Dallas* and *Dynasty*. These can be found through Google and YouTube searches.

» **View:** Cover of *The Yuppie Handbook* (Piesman & Hartley, 1984), available at http://www.citizenmag.com/2013/03/22/the-yuppie-handbook/

» **Read:** "An Ambitious Defense of Yuppies" by Bob Greene (1985), available at http://articles.chicagotribune.com/1985-05-07/features/8501280315_1_yuppies-generation-hated

» **Listen:** "Hip to Be Square" (Gibson, Hopper, & Lewis, 1986) by Huey Lewis and the News, available on YouTube.

» **Read:** *The Bonfire of the Vanities* (Wolfe, 1987/2008) excerpt, "The Master of the Universe," available at http://usatoday30.usatoday.com/life/books/excerpts/2007-04-05-bonfire-vanities_N.htm?csp=34

» **View:** Artwork from Robert Longo, available at http://www.robertlongo.com/portfolios/1030

» **View:** Multimedia artwork from Jenny Holzer, available at http://www.sfmoma.org/explore/multimedia/videos/138. Students can also read a 1988 article by Michael Brenson on Jenny Holzer and her work, available at http://www.nytimes.com/1988/08/07/arts/art-view-jenny-holzer-the-message-is-the-message.html?pagewanted=all&src=pm.

Key Terms

» *Affluence:* having much wealth, including money, property, and other material possessions
» *Yuppie:* stands for young, urban professional; referred to any young, college-educated city-dweller who had a professional career and made a substantial income

Learning Experiences

1. Explain to students that all of the trends they have discussed (e.g., Reagan's economic policies, increased defense spending in the renewed focus on the Cold War, and the growth of technology industries) led to economic growth in the United States by the mid-1980s. Have students read "The Reagan Boom" by Martin Anderson from 1990 and answer the questions on Handout 4.1 (The Material World) **Ask:** What was happening at this point in the 1980s? What changes in the United States economy does Anderson describe? What statistics does he provide? Given the economic situation of the 1970s, how do you think this growth changed America and Americans?

2. To look at the effects of these economic changes on Americans, tell the students that they are going to read from a popular novel and listen to popular songs. Have students read Chapter 3 from Tom Wolfe's (1987/2008) *The Bonfire of the Vanities* and listen to the two songs: "Material Girl" (Brown & Rans, 1984) by Madonna and "Opportunities (Let's Make Lots of Money)" (Tennant & Lowe, 1984) by the Pet Shop Boys. Discuss student responses. Show students images from the TV shows *Dallas* and *Dynasty*. **Ask:** How would you describe the attitudes and priorities of the 1980s based on these songs and the reading? Do these show a dramatic shift in American values? Why or why not? How did the growing wealth alter our priorities and identity and in what ways?

3. Explain that the media labeled the young adults who were part of this growing wealth as "yuppies." Give students Handout 4.2 (Yuppies). Put the cover of *The Yuppie Handbook* (Piesman & Hartley, 1984) up for students to see. Explain that although the book was a humorous statement about young professionals in the 1980s and portrayed a stereotype, it did reveal something about trends of the time. **Ask:** What do you see in the picture? What stands out about these people? How do they look? What are they wearing? Based on what you read, why might this be? What do they do? What do they seem to value?

4. Have students read the Bob Greene (1985) article, "An Ambitious Defense of Yuppies," and listen to "Hip to Be Square" (Gibson, Hopper, & Lewis, 1986) by Huey Lewis and the News. Discuss student responses. **Ask:** Who were the yuppies in their teens and 20s? (*Note:* Make sure students realize that the yuppies are the same generation who were protestors in college in the 1960s.) What caused this change in the yuppies? What experiences or situations changed them since their teens and 20s? Think about Sherman McCoy and Bob Greene: How did they see themselves and others like them? What identity did they create for themselves? How did others see them? Why the difference in views? Why did being socially acceptable and affluent become more important to this group of people? What was going on in American culture to explain these changing behaviors and priorities? How typical do you think this was? Why?

5. Give students Handout 4.3 (Beneath the Surface). Have students read the second excerpt from *The Bonfire of the Vanities* (Wolfe, 1987/2008), "The Master of the Universe." Have them view the art by Robert Longo and Jenny Holzer and answer the questions on the handout. Discuss student responses as a whole class. **Ask:** What was the tone and message of the art you looked at? How did it make you feel? Why do you think Jenny Holzer chose those locations for her art? What normally is in those places? How does her choice of location match the message of her art? (*Note:* Help students to understand that part of Holzer's critique of the materialism of American culture led her to take billboards and other advertising space away from corporations; she put her art on advertising signs, in bank windows, on luggage carousels, on stadium big screens, etc.)

6. Have students complete Handout 4.4 (From Ideals to Critiques). Discuss student responses. **Ask:** What can we conclude about the effects of the growing economy on America in the 1980s? Was it a "material world"? In what ways? For whom? In what ways is this an inaccurate depiction of the decade? What values were changing? What was staying the same? How would you characterize the early 1980s and the effects of the changing economy on Americans? Why?

Assessing Student Learning

» Handout 4.1 (The Material World)
» Handout 4.2 (Yuppies)
» Handout 4.3 (Beneath the Surface)
» Handout 4.4 (From Ideals to Critiques)
» Discussions

Extending Student Learning

The following are optional activities for extending student learning in this lesson:

» The "yuppie" characterized the affluence and lifestyle of young professionals during the 1980s. Have students investigate the yuppie lifestyle in more detail. This could include exploring the careers that were popular in the 1980s, television programs relating to the lifestyle, etc. Have students prepare an engaging presentation to share their findings.

» Have students research terms such as "yuppies" that refer to people of a certain age, era, or economic situation. They could examine terms such as Gen X-ers, Yippies, and DINCs. Have them share their findings, including a critical analysis of whether the terms accurately describe the various groups.

» Have students investigate the sources of the affluence in the 1980s. They could research the types of businesses that were successful then, the status of the American economy during that decade, etc. Have them present their research in chart or graph form.

HANDOUT 4.1

The Material World

Directions: Respond to these questions after reading the selections and listening to the songs.

"The Reagan Boom"

1. What changes in the United States economy does this piece describe? What evidence and data does he present?

   _____

   _____

   _____

2. Think of all the ways that this might affect the United States? What are the benefits of these changes? What drawbacks might there be? How might it affect the U.S. socially? Culturally? Politically?

   _____

   _____

   _____

The Bonfire of the Vanities

1. What details about Sherman McCoy's life are mentioned in this excerpt?

   _____

   _____

   _____

2. What is life like for the McCoys?

   _____

   _____

   _____

3. What issues seems to concern Sherman the most? What are his priorities?

   _____

   _____

   _____

4. There are several references to what is socially correct or acceptable. What do these comments reveal about Sherman and others like him?

   _____

   _____

   _____

Handout 4.1: The Material World, continued

Songs: "Material Girl" by Madonna and "Opportunities" by Pet Shop Boys

1. What are the songs concerned about?

    _____

    _____

    _____

2. How do these songs fit with the story you read about Sherman McCoy?

    _____

    _____

    _____

Summary

During the 1980s two of the most popular primetime shows were *Dallas* and *Dynasty*. *Dallas* focused on a wealthy oil tycoon and ranching families in Texas and their manipulations to increase their own wealth. *Dynasty* was about a wealthy oil tycoon family in Colorado and their luxurious lifestyle. Also, the show *Lifestyles of the Rich and Famous* debuted on TV, taking you on tours of the homes, estates, yachts, and other aspects of the world of the wealthy. What does the popularity of these shows tell us about interests and attitudes during the 1980s?

HANDOUT 4.2
Yuppies

Directions: Respond to these questions after reading the selection and listening to the song.

"An Ambitious Defense of Yuppies"

1. How does the author define "yuppie"?

    _____

    _____

    _____

2. How does he describe the actions of yuppies? How does he characterize the behavior of people like Sherman McCoy?

    _____

    _____

    _____

3. Why does he seem so defensive? How does he say others view yuppies? Are the actions of the yuppies all that different from Americans of the past—the Gilded Age, the 1920s, the 1950s? Why or why not?

    _____

    _____

    _____

4. Who were the yuppies in their teens/college years? Looking at the cover of *The Yuppie Handbook*, does the yuppie past surprise you? Why or why not?

    _____

    _____

    _____

Listen to "Hip to be Square" by Huey Lewis & the News

1. What change is being described in this song?

    _____

    _____

    _____

2. What is the message of the song? Why do you think the songwriter feels the need to say it's "hip" to be "square? What does "square" mean?

    _____

    _____

    _____

Summary

1. What caused this change in the yuppies? What experiences or situations changed them since their teens and twenties?

   _____

   _____

   _____

2. Think about Sherman McCoy and Bob Greene. How do they see themselves and others like them? What identity did they create for themselves? How do others see them? Why the difference in views?

   _____

   _____

   _____

3. Why did being socially acceptable and being affluent become more important to this group of people? What was going on in American culture to explain these changing behaviors and priorities?

   _____

   _____

   _____

HANDOUT 4.3

Beneath the Surface

Directions: Respond to these questions after reading the selection and viewing the artwork.

The Bonfire of the Vanities

1. What is Sherman trying to do now? Why?

2. What is a "Master of the Universe" in Sherman's mind? Why does Sherman feel he is one?

3. What details about his apartment and life do we get in this segment? What insights does Sherman give us about his wife and how he sees wealthy women?

4. What emotions do we see in this story? How is this image of Sherman different from the one we saw in the first excerpt? If he is a "Master of the Universe" and lives in this home, why does he feel these emotions?

5. What does this story tell us about the lives of the affluent during the 1980s?

Robert Longo's art

1. What images do you see? What feelings do you get from these images? Why?

Handout 4.3: Beneath the Surface, continued

2. How are the people in these pictures similar to *The Yuppie Handbook*? How are they different? How do these pictures compare to the image of Sherman McCoy from the last passage?

_____

_____

_____

3. What is the message of this art? What does it suggest about life for the growing affluent class in the 1980s?

_____

_____

_____

Jenny Holzer's art

1. Where do you see her art? What do you normally expect to see in these places? What message is she sending by putting her art in these places?

_____

_____

_____

2. What is the message and tone of her art? What is her point?

_____

_____

_____

3. What does Holzer say about 1980s society? How do her views compare and contrast to the idea of the Yuppie?

_____

_____

_____

Name:_____ Date:_____

HANDOUT 4.4
From Ideals to Critiques

Directions: Complete these questions about various ideas from the 1980s.

Ideal: What does the ideal of *Dynasty* and *Dallas* tell us about Americans in the 1980s? What did Americans hope for/aspire to? What did Americans seem to want or seek? Are these new goals? When in American history have we seen similar goals and aspirations? What conditions and inventions made the focus on wealthy lifestyles more pronounced in the 1980s?

Critiques: What did critics like Longo and Holzer say about this popularized wealthy lifestyle? What problems did they see? What didn't they agree with in the lifestyle of the wealthy?

Do Americans still have a fascination with wealthy lifestyles? How are our cultural traits similar to the those in the 1980s? How are we different? What criticisms do we make today of reality TV stars and celebrity lifestyles? How is that similar to the critiques we saw in the 1980s? How is it different?

Reality: What can we conclude about 1980s America from this? What values were changing in the 1980s? What values were the same from the 1970s, 1960s, and earlier? How did the tension between aspiring to wealth and the criticism of wealth shape American identity in the 1980s?

LESSON 5

The King and Queen of Pop: Michael Jackson and Madonna

Alignment of Unit Goals

» Goal 1: To understand the concept of identity in 1980s America.
» Goal 2: To develop skills in historical analysis and song and artwork interpretation.
» Goal 4: To develop an understanding of historical events occurring in the United States during the 1980s.

Unit Objectives

» To describe how the American identity changed during the 1980s.
» To describe how changes in American identity in the 1980s were revealed in the music, art, and literature of the decade.

» To define the context in which a song or piece of art was produced and the implications of context for understanding the artifact.

» To describe a writer's or artist's intent in producing a given song or piece of art based on understanding of text and context.

» Describe major historical events during the 1980s that affected the American identity.

» Describe music, art, and literature of the 1980s that reflected the American identity.

Resources for Unit Implementation

» **Handout 5.1:** Music Analysis Model

» **Handout 5.2:** Popular Music Venn Diagram

» **Handout 5.3:** Discographies of Michael Jackson and Madonna

» **Listen:** Michael Jackson's (1982a; 1982b) songs "Beat It," "Billie Jean," and "Thriller" (Temperton, 1982); and Madonna's (1983) songs "Lucky Star," "Holiday" (Hudson & Stevens, 1983), and "Borderline" (Lucas, 1983). All of the songs are available on YouTube.

» **View:** YouTube clips about Madonna, available at http://www.youtube.com/watch?v =rTYlq4czXms and http://www.youtube.com/watch?v=U6A3qmXbN1I

» **View:** Michael Jackson's 51st birthday celebration, available at http://www.youtube. com/watch?v=zATHEl_37iY

Key Terms

» *Icon:* a person regarded as a symbol of a cultural movement

» *Pop music:* an abbreviation for "popular" music; refers to music of general appeal

Learning Experiences

1. Explain that we previously talked about the rise of MTV. One effect of MTV was that people could see their favorite artists and groups in a new way, in a staged video, and more frequently than in the past. **Ask:** Why do you watch music videos? How do those videos affect you? How might seeing artists on video affect American culture and teenagers especially? What did The Buggles song, "Video Killed the Radio Star" (Downes, Horn, & Woolley, 1979), say was an effect?

2. Tell students that they will look at two influential—and controversial—artists of the 1980s: Michael Jackson and Madonna. **Ask:** Have you heard of these two musicians? What do you know about them? Which of their songs do you know? Michael Jackson is often referred to as the "King of Pop" and Madonna as the "Queen of Pop." What does this tell us about how people view these two artists?

3. Have students listen to some of the early 1980s songs by both artists. Michael Jackson's (1982a, 1982b) "Beat It," "Billie Jean," and "Thriller" (Temperton, 1982); and Madonna's (1983) "Lucky Star," "Holiday" (Hudson & Stevens, 1983), and "Borderline" (Lucas, 1983). Show the music video for one song by each artist so that the students can see the dress, dance, and performance of each. Have students complete Handout 5.1 (Music Analysis Model) for each artist's songs. **Ask:** What is your reaction to these songs? Why

do you think they were controversial in the 1980s? How did they each bring a change to American culture and music?

4. Have students view two YouTube clips from the 1980s about Madonna. **Ask:** What do you notice? Look at the fans and at the young female reporter. How are their appearances different? Do people have similar reactions to music stars today? How do you think parents reacted to kids dressing and acting this way? How different is this from the reactions we saw to Elvis in the 1950s? How is this similar to the reactions to Elvis? Was this reaction to music stars new? What age were Madonna fans? How was MTV affecting youth culture?

5. **Ask:** How do the images of these artists in the videos fit with the images of yuppies and *The Bonfire of the Vanities* (Wolfe, 1987/2008) that we looked at in the previous lesson? Do you think yuppies listened to these two artists? Why or why not? How do the images in these clips fit with the tensions we saw in the "Cyberpunk" story (Bethke, 1983)? What new individual identities were being created in the 1980s? How were the identities of adults different from those of younger people? What were the effects of this on the United States? Do we still see similar divisions today?

6. Have students compare the music of Michael Jackson and Madonna to the music they studied in earlier units. Have students complete Handout 5.2 (Popular Music Venn Diagram). You may also want to use Handout 5.3 (Discographies of Michael Jackson and Madonna) as a resource. Display student responses on the board and discuss. **Ask:** Both Madonna's and Michael Jackson's music were danced to. How is this music different from disco, which was also dance music? How are the lyrics different? How is this a continuation of the types of music we saw in the 1970s? Why are Michael Jackson and Madonna seen as so revolutionary in changing American music?

7. Show students the clip from Michael Jackson's 51st birthday celebration in Mexico, where more than 13,000 people danced to "Thriller." **Ask:** This was more than 20 years after the song "Thriller" was released. What does it tell us about the effect of Michael Jackson on music and people?

8. Have students look at the list of albums each artist has recorded (a list is provided in Handout 5.3) and have students look up the awards, both music awards and Guinness World Records, and other achievements they were awarded. **Ask:** Why have these two artists had such a long-term effect on music? Why are new artists often compared to these two musicians (e.g., Lady Gaga, who is often compared to Madonna)? What does this tell us about American culture and American identity?

9. **Ask:** At the start of the lesson, a statement was made that Michael Jackson is called the King of Pop and Madonna is called the Queen of Pop—do you feel they deserve these labels? Why or why not? What does the continued popularity of both their personas and music tell us about American identity?

Assessing Student Learning

- » Handout 5.1 (Music Analysis Model)
- » Handout 5.2 (Popular Music Venn Diagram)
- » Discussions

Extending Student Learning

The following are optional activities for extending student learning in this lesson:

» Both Madonna and Michael Jackson were controversial figures for various reasons. Have students research either musician and address why he or she was controversial, but also how he or she contributed to American music and American culture in positive ways.

» Many people would consider both Michael Jackson and Madonna to be "icons" of American pop culture. Have students consider which musician might be considered a contemporary icon of American culture and compare that person to either Jackson or Madonna. The end product should include a graphic depiction of the comparison.

» Both Michael Jackson and Madonna were inductees in the Rock and Roll Hall of Fame. Have students investigate the criteria for being selected, then write a critique of why the selection of one of the artists was or was not warranted.

HANDOUT 5.1
Music Analysis Model

Directions: Please complete the Music Analysis Chart for both Michael Jackson and Madonna songs.

Michael Jackson: Song Title: _____

What is the title of the song? Why was it given this title?

Title:
Why do you think it was given this title?
Which words in the title are especially important? Why?

What is your reaction to the song?

What is the first thing about this song that draws your attention?
What is in the song that surprises you, or that you didn't expect?
What are some of the powerful ideas expressed in the song?
What feelings does the song cause in you?
What questions does it raise for you?

When was the song written? Why was it written?

Who is the songwriter(s)?
When was the song written?
What is the song's purpose? To entertain? To dance to? To critique something?
What were the important events occurring at the time the song was written?
Who is the intended audience?
What biases do you see in the author's lyrics?

What are the important ideas in this song?

Lyrics	Music/Accompaniment
What is the subject of the song? Summarize the song.	Describe the music or melody of this song. Is it fast-paced or slow? Does it have low notes or high notes? Is it melodic or does it have lots of percussion?
What are the main points of the song? What is the song saying about the subject?	What feelings do you get from the music? Why?
What mood/values/feelings does the singer have about the topic?	How does the tone or mood of the music fit with the lyrics? Why might this be?

What is your evaluation of this song?

What new or different interpretation of this historical period does this song provide?
What does this song portray about American identity or how Americans felt at the time?

Name:_____ Date:_____

Madonna: Song Title:_____

What is the title of the song? Why was it given this title?

Title:
Why do you think it was given this title?
Which words in the title are especially important? Why?

What is your reaction to the song?

What is the first thing about this song that draws your attention?
What is in the song that surprises you, or that you didn't expect?
What are some of the powerful ideas expressed in the song?
What feelings does the song cause in you?
What questions does it raise for you?

When was the song written? Why was it written?

Who is the songwriter(s)?

Handout 5.1: Music Analysis Model, continued

When was the song written?
What is the song's purpose? To entertain? To dance to? To critique something?
What were the important events occurring at the time the song was written?
Who is the intended audience?
What biases do you see in the author's lyrics?

What are the important ideas in this song?

Lyrics	Music/Accompaniment
What is the subject of the song? Summarize the song.	Describe the music or melody of this song. Is it fast-paced or slow? Does it have low notes or high notes? Is it melodic or does it have lots of percussion?
What are the main points of the song? What is the song saying about the subject?	What feelings do you get from the music? Why?
What mood/values/feelings does the singer have about the topic?	How does the tone or mood of the music fit with the lyrics? Why might this be?

What is your evaluation of this song?

What new or different interpretation of this historical period does this song provide?
What does this song portray about American identity or how Americans felt at the time?

HANDOUT 5.2
Popular Music Venn Diagram

Directions: Compare the music of Michael Jackson and Madonna to that of the 1970s.

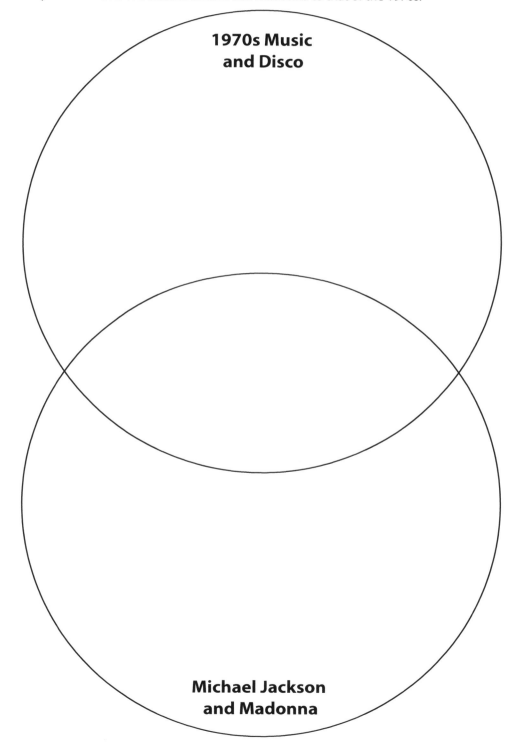

**1970s Music
and Disco**

**Michael Jackson
and Madonna**

HANDOUT 5.3

Discographies of Michael Jackson and Madonna

Michael Jackson

1972	Got To Be There
1972	Ben
1973	Music & Me
1975	Forever, Michael
1979	Off the Wall
1982	Thriller
1987	Bad
1991	Dangerous
1995	HIStory: Past, Present and Future, Book I
2001	Invincible

Madonna

1983	Madonna
1984	Like a Virgin
1986	True Blue
1987	Who's That Girl Soundtrack
1987	You Can Dance
1989	Like a Prayer
1990	I'm Breathless Soundtrack
1990	The Immaculate Collection
1992	Erotica
1994	Bedtime Stories
1996	Evita Soundtrack
1998	Ray of Light
2000	Music
2003	American Life
2005	Confessions on a Dance Floor
2008	Hard Candy
2009	Celebration
2012	MDNA

LESSON 6

The Rust Belt:
The Uneven Economy
of the 1980s

Alignment of Unit Goals

» Goal 1: To understand the concept of identity in 1980s America.
» Goal 2: To develop skills in historical analysis and song and artwork interpretation.
» Goal 3: To develop analytical and interpretive skills in literature.
» Goal 4: To develop an understanding of historical events occurring in the United States during the 1980s.

Unit Objectives

» To describe how the American identity changed during the 1980s.

» To describe how changes in American identity in the 1980s were revealed in the music, art, and literature of the decade.

» To define the context in which a song or piece of art was produced and the implications of context for understanding the artifact.

» To describe a writer's or artist's intent in producing a given song or piece of art based on understanding of text and context.

» Describe what a selected literary passage means.

» Describe major historical events during the 1980s that affected the American identity.

» Describe music, art, and literature of the 1980s that reflected the American identity.

Resources for Unit Implementation

» **Handout 6.1:** Changing Times

» **Handout 6.2:** Economic Changes in the 1980s

» **Handout 6.3:** Rust Belt Identity Chart

» **Listen:** "My Hometown" by Bruce Springsteen (1985); "Allentown" by Billy Joel (1982); "Empty Hands" by John Mellencamp (Mellencamp & Green, 1987); and "Livin' on a Prayer" (Bon Jovi, Sambora, & Child, 1986) by Bon Jovi. All of the songs available on YouTube.

» **View:** "Rust Belt" webpage, available at http://www.coalcampusa.com/rustbelt/rustbelt. htm

» **Read:** "Economic Scene; Puzzling Poverty of the 80s Boom" (Nasar, 1992), available at http://www.nytimes.com/1992/02/14/business/economic-scene-puzzling-poverty-of-the-80-s-boom.html

» **Listen:** "Down and Out in Paradise" by John Mellencamp (1987) and "Something to Believe In" (Michaels, DeVille, Dall, & Rockett, 1990) by Poison. Songs are available on YouTube.

Key Terms

» *Industry:* the businesses that manufacture a certain product or provide a specific service

» *Rust Belt:* the heavily industrial area of the Northeastern United States that had many factories

Learning Experiences

1. **Ask:** In the last few lessons, you have discussed the affluence of the 1980s. How widespread and common do you think the experience of the yuppie was? How achievable do you think the wealth and lifestyles we have looked at so far were for most Americans? Explain that in this lesson, students will look at a different perspective about life in the 1980s.

2. Give students Handout 6.1 (Changing Times). Have students listen to "My Hometown" by Bruce Springsteen (1985); "Allentown" by Billy Joel (1982); "Empty Hands" (Mellencamp &

Green, 1987) by John Mellencamp; and "Livin' on a Prayer" (Bon Jovi, Sambora, & Child, 1986) by Bon Jovi. View the "Rust Belt" webpage and have students respond to the questions. Discuss student responses as a whole class. **Ask:** What is the Rust Belt? Where is it? What caused the area's decline? (*Note:* Explain that the Northeastern United States, from New York/Pennsylvania to Michigan and Ohio, was the original center of industry and manufacturing in the U.S. By the 1980s, many of the factories were shutting down and moving to locations where production was cheaper, such as the American South and West, and to other countries like Mexico and China. This area where the industry was leaving was called the "Rust Belt.") What is the mood of the songs and pictures? What do you think were the possible effects of what you saw in the pictures? How do the lives and experiences you heard about in these songs compare to what we learned about yuppies?

3. Have students read "Economic Scene; Puzzling Poverty of the 80's Boom" (Nasar, 1992) and complete the first portion of Handout 6.2 (Economic Changes of the 1980s). **Ask:** What does this article say about the economy of the 1980s? What data does the journalist give about the economy? How does this article compare to "The Reagan Boom" (Anderson, 1990), which we read in a previous lesson? How do we get two very different descriptions of the economy of the same time? What do you think is the most accurate way to describe the 1980s economy?

4. Have students listen to "Down and Out in Paradise" by John Mellencamp (1987) and "Something to Believe In" (Michaels, DeVille, Dall, & Rockett, 1990) by Poison and complete the chart in Handout 6.2. **Ask:** What kinds of people are mentioned in these songs? What class of people? (*Note:* Help students to identify that middle-class, nonfactory workers were also being laid off and finding themselves out of work.) What are the people in these songs experiencing? What is the mood of both of these songs? What is the message of these songs? How are the experiences in these songs similar to the songs we started with? How are they different? Why was the traditional middle class also struggling in the 1980s?

5. Have students complete Handout 6.3 (Rust Belt Identity) either individually or in small groups. Discuss student responses as a whole class. **Ask:** If you have both wealthy people like the yuppies and a declining middle class in the United States at the same time, how might that affect the country?

6. Have students get in three groups. Have one group represent the upwardly mobile affluent people of the 1980s, one group represent the middle class of "Down and Out in Paradise" and "Something to Believe In," and one group represent the inhabitants of Rust Belt towns. In their groups, students should list their concerns and create a request to the government of what they would like to see it do. Each group should present its requests to the class. **Ask:** What did these groups have in common? How were they different? What should the government have done to best meet the needs of the people? Whose interests should they have listened to most? Why? What did those economic divisions do to the United States?

7. Have students write their own article or essay. Based on what they have learned in class, from their book, the songs and pictures, and the two articles, students should write a description of the 1980s economy. They should consider how they would respond to the two *New York Times* articles they read and what they feel was the economic reality of the 1980s.

Assessing Student Learning

» Handout 6.1 (Changing Times)
» Handout 6.2 (Economic Changes in the 1980s)
» Handout 6.3 (Rust Belt Identity Chart)
» Discussions

Extending Student Learning

The following are optional activities for extending student learning in this lesson:

» Have students investigate the status of the Rust Belt region today. They should report about the presence or absence of modern industry there and the economic conditions of the residents.
» In contemporary America, globalization and the emergence of new technologies are changing the workplace in significant ways, much as the availability of cheaper labor changed the Rust Belt during the 1980s. Have students investigate modern workplace trends that have affected American culture. They should share their findings in an interactive display.

Name: _____ Date: _____

HANDOUT 6.1
Changing Times

Part I: Music

Directions: Listen to the songs and respond to the questions.

Bruce Springsteen: "My Hometown"

1. What changes in the American landscape are being described? What historical details or trends that we have discussed in class are present in this song?

   _____

   _____

2. What is the point of view of this song? What is the overall mood of this song? What symbols or images are used to convey the mood?

   _____

   _____

3. What is the effect of these changes on American identity?

   _____

   _____

Billy Joel: "Allentown"

1. What changes in the American landscape are being described? What historical details or trends that we have discussed in class are present in this song?

   _____

   _____

2. What is the point of view of this song? What is the overall mood of this song? What symbols or images are used to convey the mood?

   _____

   _____

3. What does the line, "They threw an American flag in our face" mean?

   _____

   _____

4. How does he see American culture and values changing?

   _____

   _____

John Mellencamp: "Empty Hands"

1. What changes in the American landscape are being described? What historical details or trends that we have discussed in class are present in this song?

2. What is the point of view of this song? What is the overall mood of this song? What symbols or images are used to convey the mood?

3. What are people doing to survive their situations?

4. How are the situations and conditions faced by these people changing and how does that affect their values and attitudes?

Bon Jovi: "Livin' on a Prayer"

1. What changes in the American landscape are being described? What historical details or trends that we have discussed in class are present in this song?

2. What is the point of view of this song? What is the overall mood of this song? What symbols or images are used to convey the mood?

3. What is happening to these people? What changes in American experiences do we see in this song? What traits and priorities are becoming more important? Which aspects are becoming less important? Why?

Handout 6.1: Changing Times, continued

Summary

1. What similarities exist between the songs? What is happening in the songs? Why?

    _____

    _____

2. What part of the United States do these songs seem to describe?

    _____

    _____

3. In the 1970s, we were in a recession. What is different in these songs about the 1980s? How are the experiences and feelings in these songs different from what you saw in the 1970s?

    _____

    _____

Part II: Images

Directions: Listen to the songs and respond to the questions.

Go to http://www.coalcampusa.com/rustbelt/rustbelt.htm. Pick one state (West Virginia, Pennsylvania, Kentucky, Ohio, or Indiana) at the bottom of the text and view the different pages of images for that city.

1. What types of images do you see?

    _____

    _____

2. What is the mood of these pictures?

    _____

    _____

3. What might be all of the effects of what you see in these pictures? Economic effects? Cultural? For communities?

    _____

    _____

HANDOUT 6.2

Economic Changes of the 1980s

Part I: "Economic Scene; Puzzling Poverty of the 80s Boom"

Directions: Read the article and respond to the questions.

1. What does this article say about the economy of the 1980s?

   _____

   _____

2. What data does the author give about the economy?

   _____

   _____

3. How does this article compare to "The Reagan Boom," which we read previously?

   _____

   _____

4. How do we get two very different descriptions of the economy of the same time?

   _____

   _____

Part II: Music

Directions: Listen to the songs, then complete the chart.

	John Mellencamp: "Down and Out in Paradise"	Poison: "Something to Believe in"
What kinds of people are mentioned in these songs? What classes?		
What is the experience of the people in these songs?		
What is the mood of both of these songs?		
What is the message of these songs?		

HANDOUT 6.3

Rust Belt Identity Chart

Directions: Complete this chart about the identity of the American people in the 1980s.

Identity changes with new ideas, experiences, conditions, or in response to other expressions of identity
What conditions were changing in the Rust Belt region? How was this affecting the identity and circumstances of the people who lived there? What was changing about their priorities, behaviors, and traits?
Although members of a group or society may have different individual identities, they still share particular elements of identity
How did the people living in these areas feel different from the rest of America? Why? What did they have in common with other Americans, like those we have been talking about?

LESSON 7

A Rainbow Coalition:
Race in the 1980s

Alignment of Unit Goals

» Goal 1: To understand the concept of identity in 1980s America.
» Goal 2: To develop skills in historical analysis and song and artwork interpretation.
» Goal 3: To develop analytical and interpretive skills in literature.
» Goal 4: To develop an understanding of historical events occurring in the United States during the 1980s.

Unit Objectives

» To describe how the American identity changed during the 1980s.
» To describe how changes in American identity in the 1980s were revealed in the music, art, and literature of the decade.

» To define the context in which a song or piece of art was produced and the implications of context for understanding the artifact.

» To describe a writer's or artist's intent in producing a given song or piece of art based on understanding of text and context.

» To describe what a selected literary passage means.

» To describe major historical events during the 1980s that affected the American identity.

» To describe music, art, and literature of the 1980s that reflected the American identity.

Resources for Unit Implementation

» **Handout 7.1:** Where Do We Stand?

» **Handout 7.2:** "Recitatif" Questions

» **Handout 7.3:** Living in the City

» **Handout 7.4:** African American Identity in the 1980s Chart

» **Listen:** "Which Way to America?" (Reid, 1989) by Living Colour. Available on YouTube.

» **Read:** Jesse Jackson's speech at the 1984 Democratic Party National Convention, available at http://www.americanrhetoric.com/speeches/jessejackson1984dnc.htm (*Note:* The teacher can cut out portions to make it more manageable for students.)

» **View:** Artwork by Carrie Mae Weems, available at http://carriemaeweems.net/galleries/american-icons.html

» **View:** *My Calling (Cards) #1* by Adrian Piper (1986–1990), available at http://www.spencerart.ku.edu/exhibitions/radicalism/piper1.shtml

» **Read:** "Recitatif" by Toni Morrison (1983), available at http://www.nbu.bg/webs/amb/american/5/morrison/recitatif.htm

» **Read:** "Black Poverty Spreads in 50 Biggest U.S. Cities" (Herbers, 1987), available at http://www.nytimes.com/1987/01/26/us/black-poverty-spreads-in-50-biggest-us-cities.html?pagewanted=all&src=pm

» **View:** *Street Story Quilt Part I, II, III* by Faith Ringgold (1985), available at http://www.metmuseum.org/Collections/search-the-collections/485416#fullscreen

» **Listen:** Living Colour's "Open Letter (To a Landlord)" (Reid & Morris, 1989); Run–D.M.C.'s "Wake Up" (Simmons, Smith, Simmons, & Hayden, 1984), and Public Enemy's "Party for Your Right to Fight" (Ridenhour, Sadler, & Shocklee, 1987). All of the songs are available on YouTube.

Key Terms

» *Coalition:* a group of people who have joined together to achieve a common purpose

» *Integrate:* to combine something (often educational facilities or classes) that had been previously separated by race into one unified system

Learning Experiences

1. Explain to students that they have seen how the economic patterns of the 1980s affected different social classes. Play Living Colour's "Which Way to America?" (Reid, 1989). **Ask:**

What is the message of this song? What is the mood or tone of this song? What does the song suggest about economic divisions in the United States in the 1980s?

2. Tell students that they will look at other groups who faced additional challenges in American society and who were affected by the economic changes. Explain that Jesse Jackson went to Selma, AL, in 1965 to march with Dr. Martin Luther King, Jr. He went on to work with the Southern Christian Leadership Conference (SCLC) and was present at the assassination of Dr. King. In 1984, Jesse Jackson started the National Rainbow Coalition to work for equal rights. Give students a copy of Jesse Jackson's speech at the 1984 Democratic Party National Convention. Have students read the speech, view art by Carrie Mae Weems and Adrian Piper (1986–1990), and answer the questions using Handout 7.1 (Where Do We Stand?). Discuss student responses. **Ask:** What divisions did these people still see in the United States? What economic issues were African Americans facing in the 1980s? What social tensions still existed? What do these tell us about racial relations in the United States at that time? Why were these divisions so hard to overcome?

3. Explain to students that during the 1970s, there were several court cases concerning integrating schools. The problematic issue for African Americans was that students went to the school in their neighborhood, and many neighborhoods consisted of predominantly one racial group. The racial composition of neighborhoods resulted in schools being racially segregated. To solve this issue and create racially blended schools, cases like *Swann v. Charlotte-Mecklenberg* in 1971 stated that busing students could achieve racially balanced schools. School districts across the country implemented mandatory busing programs to move students to schools outside their neighborhoods in order to make sure that all schools had a mix of races in them. These programs carried on through the 1980s and even into the 1990s. Tell students that they are going to read a story by Toni Morrison (1983) that addresses this issue. Give students a copy of "Recitatif" and Handout 7.2 ("Recitatif" Questions) to complete on their own or in small groups. Discuss student responses as a whole class. **Ask:** What do the two girls in the story have in common? What differences do you see between the two girls? One of the girls is Black and the other is White. What is their initial reaction when they are put in a room together? Why? What happens when their mothers meet later in the story? What racial tensions appear in this scene? What is the debate about busing? How does Twyla feel about busing? What is Roberta's feeling about it? Why are they on different sides of the picket line? The author never tells us which girl is which race—why does she do this? What is her objective in keeping the race unknown? What does this story tell us about racial relations in the United States during the 1980s?

4. Have students read "Black Poverty Spreads in 50 Biggest U.S. Cities" from 1987 by John Herbers in *The New York Times*. **Ask:** What trend does Herbers describe in this article? What group in the U.S. is hurt the most? Why? Do you think this was the experience of all Blacks in the 1980s? Based on the article, what challenges did living in the inner city present? How did living in the inner city make it harder for residents to improve their economic conditions?

5. Give students Handout 7.3 (Living in the City). Have students view the art of Faith Ringgold (1985), *Street Story Quilt Part I, II, III*, and listen to Living Colour's "Open Letter (To a Landlord)" (Reid & Morris, 1989); Run–D.M.C.'s "Wake Up" (Simmons, Smith, Simmons, & Hayden, 1984); and Public Enemy's "Party for Your Right to Fight" (Ridenhour, Sadler, &

Shocklee, 1988). Have students answer the questions individually or in small groups and then discuss student responses as a whole class. **Ask:** When you read President Reagan's inaugural address, he talked of "no racial divisions" and a country where there would be economic opportunities for "all Americans with no barriers of . . . discrimination." Do you think these artists felt his speech had proven true? Why or why not? What is the mood of this art and music? What is the message? What did the artists want to see happen? How do you see celebration of African American culture and heritage in these works?

6. Have students complete Handout 7.4 (African American Identity Chart) on their own or in small groups. Discuss student responses as a whole class. **Ask:** What similarities do you see between the 1980s and today? What has changed since the 1980s? In the last lesson, you tried to convince the government to address the needs of one socioeconomic group in the U.S. in the 1980s. In the 1960s, the government thought building large public housing structures in the inner city for those in poverty would give them a place to live and help them improve their status. Did that work? Why or why not? Based on what you have learned in the lesson, what requests to or changes by the government do you think needed to be made in the 1980s? Why?

Assessing Student Learning

- »   Handout 7.1 (Where Do We Stand?)
- »   Handout 7.2 ("Recitatif" Questions)
- »   Handout 7.3 (Living in the City)
- »   Handout 7.4 (African American Identity in the 1980s Chart)
- »   Discussions

Extending Student Learning

The following are optional activities for extending student learning in this lesson:

- »   Have students read the op-ed "Poverty in America: Why Can't We End It?" (Edelman, 2012), available at http://www.nytimes.com/2012/07/29/opinion/sunday/why-cant-we-end-poverty-in-america.html?_r=1&adxnnl=1&pagewanted=all&adxnnlx=1382539524-kHoPfyisP/LG6MRk+kE/bA. They should discuss the title of the article and compare it to the Herbers (1987) article.
- »   Have students conduct research to find additional information about the Rainbow Coalition to share with their classmates.
- »   Have students view the movie *Ballou* (http://www.balloumovie.com), about a struggling inner-city high school near Washington, DC. Discuss the idea of "education as a civil right" for all students. Have them create proposals for improving their own school.

HANDOUT 7.1
Where Do We Stand?

Jesse Jackson's speech

Directions: Respond to these questions after reading the speech.

1. What divisions did Jackson see in the United States?

   _____

   _____

2. What is the "Rainbow Coalition"?

   _____

   _____

3. What similarities did he stress among people? What did he feel unites us?

   _____

   _____

4. What criticisms did he make about President Reagan's economic policies? Who did he feel is hurt the most?

   _____

   _____

5. Why did he argue that the Democratic Party needs Black voters?

   _____

   _____

6. What was his dream/vision for the future? What does it remind you of?

   _____

   _____

Carrie Mae Weems' art

Directions: Respond to these questions after viewing the artwork.

1. What are the subjects of Weems' art? What images do you see? Look for an object that has an African American on it. How is the person portrayed? What are they doing? Why is this object in this setting?

   _____

   _____

2. What is her message about race relations in her art?

   _____

   _____

Handout 7.1: Where Do We Stand?, continued

Adrian Piper's art

Directions: Respond to these questions after viewing the image.

1. What is her message in the card?

   _____

   _____

2. What does the fact that she has this card and feels the need to say this tell us about race relations in the U.S. in the 1980s?

   _____

   _____

Summary

Directions: Respond to the following questions.

How would you summarize the status of race relations in the United States in the early 1980s? What progress was made? What hurdles remained?

_____

_____

_____

_____

_____

_____

_____

_____

_____

_____

HANDOUT 7.2
"Recitatif" Questions

Directions: Respond to these questions after reading "Recitatif."

1. What is the relationship between Twyla and Roberta? How did they meet? When do they meet again?

_____

_____

2. How has their relationship changed over time? Why?

_____

_____

3. What do they have in common? What differences do you see between the two girls?

_____

_____

4. One of the girls is Black and the other is White. What is their reaction when they are put in a room together initially? Why?

_____

_____

5. What happens when their mothers meet later in the story? What racial tensions appear in this scene?

_____

_____

6. What is the debate about busing? How does Twyla feel about busing? What is Roberta's feeling about it? Why are they on different sides of the picket line?

_____

_____

7. Even as they picket against each other, they still reach out to one another. What is Toni Morrison's message?

_____

_____

8. The author never tells us which girl is which race. Why does she do this? What is her objective in keeping their race unknown?

_____

_____

9. What does this story tell us about racial relations in the United States during the 1980s when it was written and published?

_____

_____

HANDOUT 7.3

Living in the City

Faith Ringgold

Directions: Respond to these questions after viewing the images.

1. What are some of the images you see in the different windows? What different emotions and experiences do you see in the various windows?

_____

_____

_____

2. What historical references do you see in the windows?

_____

_____

_____

3. What is Ringgold's message? What is the mood of this art?

_____

_____

_____

Living Colour: "Open Letter to a Landlord"

Directions: Respond to these questions after listening to the music.

1. What is the topic of this song?

_____

_____

_____

2. What is the mood of the song? What do they feel is being lost?

_____

_____

_____

3. How do the images in this song compare to the Faith Ringgold quilt?

_____

_____

_____

Public Enemy: "Party for Your Right to Fight"

Directions: Respond to these questions after listening to the music.

1. What historical references do you see in this song? Who is mentioned?

_____

_____

_____

_____

2. What does this song say about the Civil Rights Movement? What has happened to it?

_____

_____

_____

_____

3. What is the message of the song?

_____

_____

_____

_____

Run–D.M.C.: "Wake Up"

Directions: Respond to these questions after listening to the music.

1. What is this song about? What issues that we have talked about do you see in this song?

_____

_____

_____

2. Why does the song advise listeners to "wake up" from the dream of a better world? What is the message in this song?

_____

_____

_____

_____

Name:_____ Date:_____

HANDOUT 7.4

African American Identity
in the 1980s

Directions: Respond to these questions about African America identity in the 1980s, and then answer the summary questions below the chart.

Identity changes with new ideas, experiences, conditions, or in response to other expressions of identity.
What conditions were changing in the African American community? How was their identity changing? How were priorities, values, and ways of life changing for African Americans in the 1980s?
Identity is created by a group, person, or outsiders, and self-created identities may be different from how others see one's self.
How do the songs and the Faith Ringgold art create an identity for the African American community? What history and values do they promote? How would you describe the African American community portrayed in the art? Based on the news articles, how did others view African Americans, especially inner-city Blacks? Why? What causes the differences?
Although members of a group or society may have different individual identities, they still share particular elements of identity
Were all African Americans experiencing the same things in the 1980s? What are the different experiences we have seen so far? What traits did all Americans share? Think about the Run–D.M.C. song and what goals and beliefs we all share.

Handout 7.4: African American Identity in the 1980s, continued

In the last lesson, you argued for the government to address the needs of one socioeconomic group in the U.S. in the 1980s. In the 1960s, the government thought building large public-housing structures in the inner city for those in poverty would give them a place to live and help them improve their status. Did that work? Why or why not?

_____

_____

_____

_____

_____

_____

_____

_____

_____

_____

_____

_____

Based on what you have learned in the lesson, what requests or changes by the government do you think need to be made? Why?

_____

_____

_____

_____

_____

_____

_____

_____

_____

_____

_____

_____

_____

LESSON 8

The Changing Face of America: New Immigration Patterns of the 1980s

Alignment of Unit Goals

» Goal 1: To understand the concept of identity in 1980s America.
» Goal 2: To develop skills in historical analysis and song and artwork interpretation.
» Goal 3: To develop analytical and interpretive skills in literature.
» Goal 4: To develop an understanding of historical events occurring in the United States during the 1980s.

Unit Objectives

» To describe how the American identity changed during the 1980s.
» To describe how changes in American identity in the 1980s were revealed in the music, art, and literature of the decade.

» To define the context in which a song or piece of art was produced and the implications of context for understanding the artifact.

» To describe a writer's or artist's intent in producing a given song or piece of art based on understanding of text and context.

» To describe what a selected literary passage means.

» To describe major historical events during the 1980s that affected the American identity.

» To describe music, art, and literature of the 1980s that reflected the American identity.

Resources for Unit Implementation

» **Handout 8.1:** A Hispanic Perspective

» **Handout 8.2:** An Asian Perspective

» **Handout 8.3:** A Native American Perspective

» **Handout 8.4:** Ethnic Identities in the United States

» **View:** *Time* magazine's July 1985 cover, "The Changing Face of America," available at http://content.time.com/time/magazine/0,9263,7601850708,00.html

» **View:** American immigration graph, available at http://www.washingtonpost.com/wp-srv/special/national/the-state-of-immigration/

» **Read:** Excerpts from Sandra Cisneros' (1984/1991) *The House on Mango Street* (Read the chapters "The House on Mango Street," "My Name," "Those Who Don't," "Alicia Who Sees Mice," "Geraldo No Last Name," "No Speak English," "Bums in the Attic," "A Smart Cookie," and "Alicia and I Talking on Edna's Steps."). The book should be available in the school library; if not, be sure to request it ahead of time.

» **Read:** An excerpt from Amy Tan's (1989/2006) *The Joy Luck Club*. (Read the chapter entitled, "Waverly Jong: Rules of the Game."). The book should be available in the school library; if not, be sure to request it ahead of time.

» **View:** Yolanda Lopez's (1984) artwork, *Things I Never Told My Son About Being a Mexican*, available at http://archive.newmuseum.org/index.php/Detail/Object/Show/object_id/3717

» **View:** Yong Soon Min's (1989; 1984) artwork, "Make Me," available at http://www.yongsoonmin.com/art/make-me-all/, and "Back of the Bus 1953," available at http://www.yongsoonmin.com/art/back-of-the-bus-1953/

» **View:** Artwork by Edgar Heap of Birds, available at http://multiculturalcenter.osu.edu/posts/documents/edgarreading101.pdf (*Note:* It's not necessary for students to read the accompanying essay.)

Key Terms

» *Immigrant:* a person who comes from one country to live in another

» *Indigenous:* native to a certain region or country

» *Sovereignty:* independent power in government claimed by a certain group

Learning Experiences

1. Show students the *Time* magazine cover from July 1985, "The Changing Face of America," and the graph of American immigration at *The Washington Post*. **Ask:** Who were the major immigrant groups coming to the U.S. in the second half of the 20th century? How was this different from before World War II? We have talked about Hispanic Americans in the 1960s and 1970s—what do you remember about the experience of Hispanic Americans up to the 1980s?

2. Have students review the statistics at *The Washington Post* on both Latin American and Asian immigration. **Ask:** How do you think these changing immigration patterns affected the U.S.? How do you think they affected the people who immigrated here?

3. Divide the class in half. Have one half of the class read excerpts from Sandra Cisneros' (1984/1991) *The House on Mango Street* and view Yolanda Lopez's (1984) artwork, *Things I Never Told My Son About Being a Mexican*, and then answer the questions as a group on Handout 8.1 (A Hispanic Perspective). Have the other half of the class read a chapter from Amy Tan's (1989/2006) *The Joy Luck Club* and view the art of Yong Soon Min (1989; 1984), and then answer the questions as a group on Handout 8.2 (An Asian Perspective).

4. Create new small groups; each group should include several members who read Sandra Cisneros and several members who read Amy Tan. Group members should share what they read with the others in their group who read the other book. In their small groups, have them make a list of similarities and a list of the differences between Sandra Cisnero/Yolanda Lopez and Amy Tan/Yong Soon Min. **Ask:** What were common experiences of the new immigrant groups? What did different ethnicities experience differently? Discuss their responses as a whole class. What challenges did all immigrants face in coming to the United States? How were their experiences similar to the situations faced by inner-city African Americans from the last lesson? How were they different?

5. Explain that another minority group facing changing circumstances in the United States in the 1980s was the Native Americans. Explain that in 1978, Congress passed the Federal Acknowledgement Program that allowed Native American tribes without reservations to petition the government for recognition. If a tribe could meet certain qualifications, the tribe would be federally recognized and receive services from the government. Some tribes sought recognition and other tribes were recognized separately by Congress. In the 1980 case, *U.S. v. Sioux Nation of Indians*, the Supreme Court compensated the Sioux for the loss of the Black Hills in 1877. In the 1982 court case, *Seminole Tribe v. Butterworth*, the Supreme Court recognized indigenous sovereignty by allowing the Seminole to have legal gaming in Florida and paved the way for American Indian gaming sites, which provided revenue to tribes. By 1990, Congress passed the Native American Languages Act, which tried to "preserve, protect, and promote" Native American languages and the Native Americans' right to use their language anywhere, including in schools. **Ask:** What effect do you think this had on Native Americans? Why?

6. Have students view the art of Edgar Heap of Birds and answer the questions on Handout 8.3 (A Native American Perspective) in small groups. Discuss student responses as a whole class. **Ask:** Why did Edgar Heap of Birds have certain words written backwards?

7. Give students Handout 8.4 (Ethnic Identities in the United States) to complete in small groups. Discuss student responses as a whole class. **Ask:** What struggles or challenges did all of the groups we looked at face? How would you describe the experience of immi-

grants in the U.S. in the 1980s? Do you think the immigrant experience today is similar or different from what you read? Why? In what ways? What can we learn about how we interact with new immigrants from this?

Assessing Student Learning

- » Handout 8.1 (A Hispanic Perspective)
- » Handout 8.2 (An Asian Perspective)
- » Handout 8.3 (A Native American Perspective)
- » Handout 8.4 (Ethnic Identities in the United States)
- » Discussions

Extending Student Learning

The following are optional activities for extending student learning in this lesson:

- » Have students read one of the entire novels: Sandra Cisneros' (1984/1991) *The House on Mango Street* or Amy Tan's (1989/2006) *The Joy Luck Club*. Based on research they conduct about the given culture, the students should write book reviews in which they critique the book's portrayal of the culture in the selection.
- » Have students research any of the legislation of the 1980s that addressed the concerns of the various ethnic groups in the United States. Have each student focus on one law and its impact on the culture.

HANDOUT 8.1
A Hispanic Perspective

Literature

Directions: Respond to the following questions about *The House on Mango Street*.

1. What is Esperanza's neighborhood like in her eyes? How do others view her neighborhood? Why is there a difference?

_____

_____

_____

2. What types of interactions and relations between Hispanics and Whites do we see in the story?

_____

_____

_____

3. What goals and aspirations do Esperanza, Alicia, and Esperanza's mother have? How do they feel they can achieve them?

_____

_____

_____

4. What connections do Alicia, Mamacita, and Geraldo have with their homelands? What does this tell us about the experience of immigrants in the U.S.?

_____

_____

_____

5. What are the two different depictions of Geraldo? What does this reveal about the obstacles immigrants face?

_____

_____

_____

6. Esperanza repeatedly talks of wanting to leave Mango Street. Why? What does this tell us about the immigrant experience?

_____

_____

_____

Art

Directions: Respond to the following questions about Yolanda Lopez's artwork.

1. What images do you see in her art?

_____

_____

_____

2. What is the mood expressed by the art? What emotions do you experience when viewing the art?

_____

_____

_____

3. How do the titles affect your interpretation of the art?

_____

_____

_____

4. What is the message in her art? What does it tell us about the experience of immigrants in the U.S.?

_____

_____

_____

HANDOUT 8.2
An Asian Perspective

Literature

Directions: Respond to the questions about *The Joy Luck Club*.

1. What is Meimei's neighborhood like in her eyes? How do others view her neighborhood? Why is there a difference?

_____

_____

_____

2. What types of interactions and relations between Chinese and Whites do we see in the story?

_____

_____

_____

3. What "wisdoms" is Meimei's mother trying to teach her children? Why? What is her purpose? What aspirations does she have?

_____

_____

_____

4. What are "American rules" according to Meimei's mother? How does Meimei's mother view these rules? What does this tell us about the immigrant experience in the U.S.?

_____

_____

_____

5. How does playing chess create tension in Meimei's family? How do "American rules" affect Meimei?

_____

_____

_____

6. What happens at the end of the story? Why? What causes the tension between Meimei and her mother? How typical do you think this is for immigrant families?

_____

_____

_____

Name:_____ Date:_____

Art

Directions: Respond to the questions about Yong Soon Min's artwork.

1. What images do you see in her art?

    _____

    _____

    _____

2. What is the mood expressed by the art? What emotions do you experience when viewing the art?

    _____

    _____

    _____

3. How do the titles affect your interpretation of the art?

    _____

    _____

    _____

4. What is the message in her art? What does it tell us about the experience of immigrants in the U.S.?

    _____

    _____

    _____

HANDOUT 8.3

A Native American Perspective

Directions: Respond to the questions about Edgar Heap of Birds' artwork.

1. What do you see? What emotions do you experience when viewing the art?

_____

_____

_____

_____

_____

2. What is the message of this art?

_____

_____

_____

_____

_____

3. Why are certain words backwards? What is his objective in doing this?

_____

_____

_____

_____

_____

4. How is this art similar to Jenny Holzer's art? Why might he choose this way of displaying his art?

_____

_____

_____

_____

_____

Name: _____ Date: _____

HANDOUT 8.4

Ethnic Identities in the U.S.A.

Directions: Respond to the following questions about ethnic identity in the U.S. in the 1980s.

Identity changes with new ideas, experiences, and conditions, or in response to other expressions of identity.
What new situations and experiences are Meimei and Esperanza facing? How is it affecting their identity? How are they changing and becoming different from their family?

Identity is created by a group, person, or outsiders, and self-created identities may be different from how others see one's self.
How do Whites see immigrant groups and Native Americans? What identities do Whites construct of the new immigrants? How do the images Whites have of immigrants match the reality of these immigrant groups? How do these preconceived notions of immigrants create challenges for immigrants in blending in and achieving their goals?

There are multiple elements of identity and at different times, different elements have greater or lesser importance.
As Esperanza and Meimei live in the U.S., what aspects of identity are becoming more important to them? What does each girl want for herself? What aspects of their identity do they try to downplay or feel are less important? What role does their native culture play in their lives?

Handout 8.4: Ethnic Identity in the U.S.A., continued

Although members of a group or society may have different individual identities, they still share particular elements of identity.
What traits, values, and beliefs do the immigrants and Native Americans share with the rest of the Americans we have looked at in the 1980s?

Summary

Based on what you have read, what struggles did immigrants and minority groups face in the United States in the 1980s?

_____

_____

_____

_____

_____

_____

_____

_____

How would you describe the experience of immigrants to the United States in the 1980s?

_____

_____

_____

_____

_____

_____

_____

_____

The Reagan Doctrine: Involvement of the United States in World Affairs

Alignment of Unit Goals

» Goal 1: To understand the concept of identity in 1980s America.
» Goal 2: To develop skills in historical analysis and song and artwork interpretation.
» Goal 3: To develop analytical and interpretive skills in literature.
» Goal 4: To develop an understanding of historical events occurring in the United States during the 1980s.

Unit Objectives

» To describe how the American identity changed during the 1980s.
» To describe how changes in American identity in the 1980s were revealed in the music, art, and literature of the decade.
» To define the context in which a song or piece of art was produced and the implications of context for understanding the artifact.
» To describe a writer's or artist's intent in producing a given song or piece of art based on understanding of text and context.
» To describe what a selected literary passage means.
» To describe major historical events during the 1980s that affected the American identity.
» To describe music, art, and literature of the 1980s that reflected the American identity.

Resources for Unit Implementation

» **Handout 9.1:** Standing by Our Democratic Allies
» **Handout 9.2:** United States Foreign Involvement
» **Handout 9.3:** Identity Chart
» **Read:** Information about the Reagan Doctrine, available at: http://www.princeton. edu/~achaney/tmve/wiki100k/docs/Reagan_Doctrine.html
» **Listen:** "Nicaragua" by Bruce Cockburn (1984); "Please Forgive Us" (Buck & Merchant, 1989) by 10,000 Maniacs; "Lives in the Balance" by Jackson Browne (1986); and "The Big Stick" (Boon, 1985) by Minutemen. All of the songs are available on YouTube.
» **View:** "We Are the World" music video, available at http://www.youtube.com/ watch?v=M9BNoNFKCBI
» **Listen:** "Hands Across America" (Blatte, Carney, & Gottlieb, 1986), available on YouTube
» **Listen:** "Man in the Mirror" (Ballard & Garrett, 1988) by Michael Jackson; "Another Day in Paradise" by Phil Collins (1989); and "One World (Not Three)" (Sting, 1981) by The Police. All of the songs available on YouTube.
» **Read:** Excerpt from Robert Fulghum's (1988/2004) *All I Really Needed to Know I Learned in Kindergarten*, available at http://www.peace.ca/kindergarten.htm

Key Terms

» *Apartheid:* a policy of racial segregation formerly practiced in the Republic of South Africa
» *Protest:* a display of disapproval in objection to something that one is powerless to prevent or avoid

Learning Experiences

1. Have students read information on President Reagan's foreign policy, known as the Reagan Doctrine, during his second term as president. **Ask:** How would you summa-

rize President Reagan's policies during his presidency? What was the government doing? Where? Why? What was the overall purpose?

2. Break students into seven groups. Assign each group one place in the world where the United States was involved during the 1980s (e.g., Lebanon, Grenada, Libya, Nicaragua, Guatemala, South Africa, El Salvador). Have students briefly research the United States' involvement in the country they have been assigned during the 1980s. Students can use Handout 9.1 (Standing by Our Democratic Allies) to help structure their research.

3. Have each group report its findings to the class. Using the textbook, briefly review the Iran-Contra affair. Explain that people within the government were selling weapons to Iran and using the money to aid the Contra movement in Nicaragua, all without the knowledge of the American people or Congress. Lieutenant Colonel Oliver North was put on trial for his role in carrying out this plan in 1987. **Ask:** Why was the government doing all of this? How did these policies fit with the ideas from President Reagan that we read in his "evil empire" speech earlier in the decade? How do you expect Americans reacted when they found out about these actions? Based on what we have seen in the 1960s and 1970s, how do you think the public felt about this and what did they do in response?

4. Give students Handout 9.2 (United States Foreign Involvement). Have students listen to "Nicaragua" by Bruce Cockburn (1984); "Please Forgive Us" (Bulk & Merchant, 1989) by 10,000 Maniacs; "Lives in the Balance" by Jackson Browne (1986); and "The Big Stick" (Boon, 1985) by Minutemen and answer the questions either individually or in small groups. Discuss student responses as a whole class. **Ask:** What are the tone and messages of these songs? How do these songs compare to the songs about the Vietnam War in the 1960s? How were the messages the same? Different? How were the moods the same? Different? What or who was the subject of these songs? What or who was the subject of most of the Vietnam protest songs? How did these songs view the government? How is that similar to or different from the views of the government during the Vietnam protests? What does the mood and message of these songs tell us about Americans in the 1980s? Did the American public support the government's actions in less developed countries? Why or why not?

5. Explain to students that in the 1980s, the United States and other governments were putting pressure on South Africa to end its policy of apartheid, and the global news was covering famines throughout the continent of Africa. Tell students that in 1985, 47 American musical artists joined together as "U.S.A. for Africa" and recorded the song "We Are the World" (Blatte, Carney, & Gottlieb, 1986) to raise awareness and money to fight hunger in Africa. Have students view the video. See how many artists whose songs they have studied they can identify in the video. (*Note:* Students may have to go back to artists they studied in the 1960s and 1970s because Bob Dylan, Paul Simon, Diana Ross, and others all appear.)

6. Tell students that the U.S.A. for Africa album and its second fundraiser, "Hands Across America," where people paid $10 to join hands into one continuous line of people across the country, raised almost $100 million. **Ask:** What is your reaction to the song and video? What is the message of the song? What can we conclude by the fact that 47 very influential and popular musicians would come together to do this? How widespread or popular do you think this cause was? Do you think most Americans supported it? What does it tell us about Americans that people were taking these kinds of actions on their

own and not relying on the government? What values were becoming more important in America? Why was happening?

7. Have students listen to and/or watch the music videos for "Man in the Mirror" (Ballard & Garrett, 1988) by Michael Jackson; "Another Day in Paradise" by Phil Collins (1989); and "One World (Not Three)" (Sting, 1981) by The Police. Have students read an excerpt from Robert Fulghum's (1988/2004) *All I Really Needed to Know I Learned in Kindergarten*. Tell students that Robert Fulghum's book came out in 1988, and very popular posters, greeting cards, and magnets were made featuring lines from the first essay in the book. Have students answer the questions on Handout 9.2 (United States Foreign Involvement). Discuss student responses as a whole class. **Ask:** Who are these songs about? What is the message of these songs? What is the mood of the songs? Thinking about the economic issues and trends that we have looked at, do these songs surprise you? Why or why not? How does the message of these songs fit with President Reagan's "evil empire" speech and his policies? How do these songs fit with the efforts of U.S.A. for Africa? What was changing in the United States? Why? What became more of a priority in America? What situations and developments caused these changes? How did Americans see their role in the world? How was this similar to the past? How was it a change? In what ways?

8. Tell students they are going to reflect on the changes of the 1980s by completing an identity chart of Americans at the end of the 1980s. Give students Handout 9.3 (Identity Chart) and have them complete it in small groups. Discuss student responses as a whole group. **Ask:** Get out your identity wheel from the start of the decade. What is similar? What is different? How can you explain these similarities and differences? What new experiences and conditions did Americans face over the decade? How do these events and experiences explain the differences? What remained the same? What does that tell us about what it means to be an American? Early in the decade we listened to Lee Greenwood (1984) sing "God Bless the USA." Do you think those ideas still held true at the end of the decade? Why or why not?

Assessing Student Learning

» Handout 9.1 (Standing by Our Democratic Allies)
» Handout 9.2 (United States Foreign Involvement)
» Handout 9.3 (Identity Chart)
» Discussions

Extending Student Learning

The following are optional activities for extending student learning in this lesson:
» Have students research the involvement of the American government and efforts to cover up involvement in the Iran-Contra Affair. Have them focus on how the role of the executive branch operated and under what type of authorization. Students should share their findings with an analysis of the roles and limits of each branch of the American government.

» Students can investigate the end of apartheid in South Africa and the resulting changes in that society. Have students share their research in the form of a display focusing on modern-day South Africa, its government, and its culture.

» Have students consider "We Are the World" and "Hands Across America" as the basis for a fundraiser. Have them develop an idea for such a fundraiser that could be carried out on a much smaller scale locally. (Students may want to try to implement the idea, if it is a viable one.)

HANDOUT 9.1

Standing by Our Democratic Allies

Directions: Use this handout to help structure your research about one of the American allies during the 1980s.

My country is:_____

Where in the world is this country? What continent? What region of the world?
When does the U.S. get involved and for how long?
What was going on in this country that caused the U.S. to get involved? What were the events and situations that led to the United States interest in this country?
How is the United States involved? What kinds of actions by the U.S. do we see?

Handout 9.1: Standing by Our Democratic Allies, continued

What happens when the U.S. gets involved in this country?

Who is affected and in what ways?

Why is the United States getting involved in these ways in this country?

HANDOUT 9.2

United States
Foreign Involvement

Directions: Respond to these questions about the U.S.'s involvement in foreign affairs, as described in songs and books.

"Nicaragua" by Bruce Cockburn

1. What is the topic of this song?

   _____

   _____

2. What is the mood or emotion of the song?

   _____

   _____

3. What is the message about the U.S.'s involvement in Nicaragua?

   _____

   _____

"Please Forgive Us" by 10,000 Maniacs

1. Who is the "we" in this song? Who are they asking forgiveness from?

   _____

   _____

2. How does this song view the actions of the U.S. government? Why?

   _____

   _____

3. What is the message of the song?

   _____

   _____

"Lives in the Balance" by Jackson Browne

1. Whose lives are in the balance in this song?

   _____

   _____

2. How does this song view the government? Why?

_____

_____

3. What is the message of the song? What is it asking?

_____

_____

"The Big Stick" by Minutemen

1. What historic event or person does the "Big Stick" refer to?

_____

_____

2. How does this song view the actions of the U.S. government? Why?

_____

_____

3. What do they want to see happen? Why?

_____

_____

"We Are the World" by U.S.A. for Africa

1. What does the title of the song mean?

_____

_____

2. What is the message of the song?

_____

_____

3. What can we conclude by the fact that 47 musicians—very influential and popular musicians—would come together to do this?

_____

_____

"One World (Not Three)" by The Police

1. What is the title a reference to? What does it mean?

_____

_____

Handout 9.2: United States Foreign Involvement, continued

2. Who are "we" and who are "they" in the song?

_____

_____

3. What is the message of the song? How is the message similar to that of "We Are the World"?

_____

_____

"Another Day in Paradise" by Phil Collins

1. What is happening in the song? Whom is it about?

_____

_____

2. What is the message of the song?

_____

_____

3. How does this song fit with the economic issues we have looked at in the 1980s?

_____

_____

"Man in the Mirror" by Michael Jackson

1. Who/what kind of people does he mention in this song?

_____

_____

2. What is the message of the song?

_____

_____

3. What does it imply about Americans in the 1980s that he is telling them "if you want to make the world a better place . . ."?

_____

_____

All I Really Needed to Know I Learned in Kindergarten by Robert Fulghum

1. What kinds of things did he "learn"?

    _____

    _____

2. What is the message of the poem? Why does he use kindergarten for the poem?

    _____

    _____

3. Why might these ideas and this poem/book be appealing to people in the 1980s?

    _____

    _____

4. What does this tell us about values and beliefs in the United States during the 1980s?

    _____

    _____

Summary

1. How are these attitudes different from what we saw in the 1960s and 1970s?

    _____

    _____

2. How do the messages of these songs fit with President Reagan's "evil empire" speech and his policies?

    _____

    _____

3. How do these songs fit with the efforts of U.S.A. for Africa?

    _____

    _____

HANDOUT 9.3
Identity Chart

Directions: Complete the chart based on ideas that you learned in this lesson.

	Time and Place Where was the country in the late 1980s? How did this differ from the early 1980s?
Identity	**Culture and Traditions** What are the shared values, beliefs, and ways of lives of Americans by the end of the 1980s?
	History and Myths What historical events and experiences were important to Americans? How were the events of the 1980s a continuation of past trends? How was America in the 1980s changing direction from the past? What events and figures from the American past were referred to in the 1980s? What historical events and patterns were important in the 1980s?

Handout 9.3: Identity Chart, continued

Identity

International Role

What was the U.S.'s international role? How was the U.S. interacting with other countries? What was America's priority globally? How was America's role in the world changing? What was happening to the U.S.'s relationship with the Soviets? What was the U.S.'s relationship with other countries? How were nongovernment groups shaping world events?

Economy

How would you describe the economic state of the U.S. by the end of the 1980s? What types of jobs did most people have? How was wealth distributed in society?

Civic Identity

How was the role of American citizens changing? What new ways did Americans have to participate in political affairs? How did people's rights and responsibilities as citizens changed in the 1980s? Who increased their civic role? How did people feel about their ability to change government?

Race/Ethnicity

How did patterns of ethnicity change? What was the status of race relations? What improved? What challenges remained? What was the ethnic makeup of the country? How did minorities see themselves?

LESSON 10

The End of the Cold War and the 1980s

Alignment of Unit Goals

» Goal 1: To understand the concept of identity in 1980s America.
» Goal 2: To develop skills in historical analysis and song and artwork interpretation.
» Goal 3: To develop analytical and interpretive skills in literature.
» Goal 4: To develop an understanding of historical events occurring in the United States during the 1980s.

Unit Objectives

» To describe how the American identity changed during the 1980s.
» To describe how changes in American identity in the 1980s were revealed in the music, art, and literature of the decade.

» To define the context in which a song or piece of art was produced and the implications of context for understanding the artifact.

» To describe a writer's or artist's intent in producing a given song or piece of art based on understanding of text and context.

» To describe what a selected literary passage means.

» To describe major historical events during the 1980s that affected the American identity.

» To describe music, art, and literature of the 1980s that reflected the American identity.

Resources for Unit Implementation

» **Handout 10.1:** The Melting of the Cold War

» **Handout 10.2:** Identity in 1989

» **Listen:** "Leningrad" by Billy Joel (1989); "Nikita" (John & Taupin, 1985) by Elton John; and "Word of Mouth" (Rutherford & Neil, 1991) by Mike and the Mechanics. All of the songs are available on YouTube.

» **View:** Music video for "Land of Confusion" (Rutherford, Banks, & Collins, 1986) by Genesis, available at http://www.youtube.com/watch?v=zU9lv_WqK6k.

» **Read:** President Reagan's (1987) speech at Brandenburg Gate in West Berlin, available at http://www.reagan.utexas.edu/archives/speeches/1987/061287d.htm

Key Terms

» *Glasnost:* a policy that called for increased openness and transparency in government activities in the Soviet Union

» *Perestroika:* referred to the restructuring of the Soviet economic and political systems initiated by Mikhail Gorbachev in 1986

Learning Experiences

1. **Ask:** In the last lesson we talked about United States involvement around the world. Why was this happening? What was President Reagan's purpose for getting involved in these places? We read President Reagan's remarks about the Soviet Union, and he increased defense spending to prevent an expansion of Soviet power in the world. Based on what we have been studying, do you think most Americans supported his policies toward the Soviet Union? Why or why not?

2. Give students Handout 10.1 (The Melting of the Cold War). Have students listen to the songs "Leningrad" by Billy Joel (1989); "Nikita" (John & Taupin, 1985) by Elton John; and "Word of Mouth" (Rutherford & Neil, 1991) by Mike and the Mechanics. Watch the video for "Land of Confusion" (Rutherford, Banks, & Collins, 1986) by Genesis and answer the questions. Discuss student responses as a whole class. **Ask:** Based on these songs, why was the Cold War diminishing in intensity? Why did the American public no longer support the Cold War? How did Americans view Russians? Was there a fear or hatred of Russians? How might the sentiments of these songs explain how the Cold War could suddenly end?

3. Using your textbook, explain to students that during the mid-1980s, the Soviet Union experienced several changes. In 1985, Mikhail Gorbachev became the leader of the Soviet Union. The Soviet economy struggled with a shortage of consumer goods and a need to be updated. Gorbachev introduced the reforms of *glastnost* and *perestroika*. *Glastnost*, or "openness," allowed more debate and freedom of speech to reduce corruption in government. *Perestroika* means "restructuring;" Gorbachev introduced some economy reforms, including some capitalist elements, to help stimulate the economy. In 1987, President Reagan and Gorbachev agreed to an Intermediate-Range Nuclear Forces Treaty, which eliminated intermediate and short-range nuclear missiles. Later that year, President Reagan traveled to the divided city of Berlin and gave a speech in West Berlin, which could be heard through microphones and speakers in East Berlin. (*Note:* Explain to students that after the collapse of Germany at the end of World War II, the separation of Berlin began. Initially, the country was divided into four zones, where each superpower controlled a zone. When agreements broke down between the Soviet Union and the Western zones, the response of the Western leaders was to merge the French, British, and American zones in 1947, which later became West Berlin. The Soviet Union's leaders feared this union because it gave the combined zone more power than its zone. When the Western powers introduced a new form of currency into the Western zones, the Soviet Union imposed the Berlin Blockade. This divided Germany into two different governmental entities. The leadership in East Germany built the Berlin Wall, which physically divided the country into eastern communism and western democracy.

4. Have students read President Reagan's speech at Brandenburg Gate in July of 1987 and answer the questions on Handout 10.1 (The Melting of the Cold War). Discuss student responses. **Ask:** How had President Reagan's mood changed since his first inaugural address? Why was this? How did the changes Gorbachev implemented affect Americans and the United States? How long had the Cold War been going on? Explain to students that 2 years after the speech, in 1989, the Berlin Wall was taken down, and in 1991, the Soviet Union started to collapse, ending the Cold War. How did this affect the United States? The focus of American foreign policy for 50 years had been stopping the spread of communism and the Soviets—how did it change American political activity, economics, and culture for that to no longer exist? How did the United States have to change its role in the world economically and politically as global relations changed post-Soviet Union? What do you think the future (i.e., the 1990s) held for the U.S.?

5. Have students present their projects from Lesson 1. **Ask:** What similarities are in your projects? How are they different? Why is this?

6. To summarize what they have learned in this unit, have students complete Handout 10.2 (Identity in 1989) in small groups. Discuss student responses as a whole class.

Assessing Student Learning

» Handout 10.1 (The Melting of the Cold War)
» Handout 10.2 (Identity in 1989)
» Discussions
» Unit project and presentation

Extending Student Learning

The following are optional activities for extending student learning in this lesson:

» Have students research how the policies of *perestroika* and *glasnost* changed everyday life for people in the Soviet Union. Students should share their findings in a multimedia presentation.

» Have students watch the movie *The Singing Revolution*, which they may request through the school library. Have them write an essay describing how the people of Estonia used music as a part of their fight for independence from the Soviet Union.

» Have students investigate other historical movements in which individuals used music, art, or literature as a means of expressing themselves and progressing toward change.

HANDOUT 10.1
The Melting of the Cold War

Directions: Respond to these questions about the ending of the Cold War, as described in songs and a speech.

"Leningrad" by Billy Joel

1. What historic events are mentioned in the song?

    _____

    _____

2. What is Viktor's life like?

    _____

    _____

3. How is life for American kids different from Viktor's life?

    _____

    _____

4. What happens at the end of the song? What is the message of this song?

    _____

    _____

5. What does this song suggest about how Americans viewed the Cold War?

    _____

    _____

"Nikita" by Elton John

1. What is going on in this song?

    _____

    _____

2. What is he looking forward to?

    _____

    _____

3. What does this song suggest about how Americans viewed Russians and the Cold War?

    _____

    _____

Handout 10.1: The Melting of the Cold War, continued

"Word of Mouth" by Mike and the Mechanics

1. Who does the song mean we should look out for? What is the party line?

   _____

   _____

2. What does the song tell people to do?

   _____

   _____

3. What does this song suggest about how people viewed the Cold War by the late 1980s?

   _____

   _____

"Land of Confusion" by Genesis

1. Which world leaders or other influential figures were in the video?

   _____

   _____

2. What is the "land of confusion"? What causes it?

   _____

   _____

3. What is the message and mood of the song?

   _____

   _____

President Reagan's Speech at Brandenburg Gate

1. How does he describe the West and its goals?

   _____

   _____

2. How does he describe the East?

   _____

   _____

3. How does he view the relationship between the East and West?

   _____

   _____

Handout 10.1: The Melting of the Cold War, continued

4. What does he say is his goal and vision for the future? What is he trying to achieve and how?

_____

_____

5. How does he describe American intentions and actions around the world?

_____

_____

6. What demands and invitations does he make of President Gorbachev? Why does he address President Gorbachev when the Wall is controlled by the East German government?

_____

_____

HANDOUT 10.2

Identity in 1989

Directions: Respond to these questions about the American identity in 1989.

Identity changes with new ideas, experiences, conditions, or in response to other expressions of identity.
Throughout the 1980s, what new technologies, situations, and conditions did the United States encounter? What changed for Americans?
What new values, beliefs, attitudes, ways of life, and views did we see in America by 1989? Think about the identity chart you filled out in the last lesson. How is it different from the chart you started with at the beginning of the decade?
Identity is created by a group, person, or outsiders, and self-created identities may be different from how others see one's self.
How did Americans see themselves by the end of the decade? How did we view our role in the world?
How did the American view of themselves affect how the U.S. proceeded as the Soviet Union ceased to exist and world relations began to change?
How do you think other countries viewed the U.S. by the end of the decade?

Handout 10.2: Identity in 1989, continued

There are multiple elements of identity and at different times, different elements have greater or lesser importance.
Which elements of identity became more important during the 1980s? What priorities increased? What became less of a priority? Why?
Although members of a group or society may have different individual identities, they still share particular elements of identity.
What groups in the U.S. had unique identities? What elements of identity divided or set apart groups within American society?   What traits, values, and traditions did Americans at the end of the 1980s have in common despite their differences?

Summary

How would you summarize the 1980s? What was the decade all about and what were the major trends? How did the events of this decade shape the United States and us today?

_____

_____

_____

_____

_____

_____

_____

_____

References

Anderson, M. (1990). *The Reagan boom*. Retrieved from http://www.nytimes.com/1990/01/17/opinion/the-reagan-boom-greatest-ever.html

B-52's. (1989). Channel z. On *Cosmic thing* [CD]. Los Angeles, CA: Reprise.

Ballard, G., & Garrett, S. (1988). Man in the mirror [Recorded by Michael Jackson]. On *Bad* [CD]. New York, NY: Epic. (1987)

Bethke, B. (1983). *Cyberpunk*. Retrieved from http://www.infinityplus.co.uk/stories/cpunk.htm

Blatte, M., Carney, H., & Gottlieb, L. (1986). We are the world [Performed by U.S.A. for Africa]. On *Hands across America* [CD]. Hands Across America.

Bon Jovi, J., Sambora, R., & Child, D. (1986). Livin' on a prayer [Recorded by Bon Jovi]. On *Slippery when wet* [CD]. New York, NY: Mercury.

Boon, D. (1985). The big stick [Recorded by Minutemen]. On *3-way tie (for last)* [Record]. Long Beach, CA: SST.

Brown, P., & Rans, R. (1984). Material girl [Recorded by Madonna]. On *Like a virgin* [Record]. Los Angeles, CA: Warner Bros.

Brenson, M. (1988, August 7). *Art view; Jenny Holzer: The message is the message*. Retrieved from http://www.nytimes.com/1988/08/07/arts/art-view-jenny-holzer-the-message-is-the-message.html?pagewanted=all&src=pm

Browne, J. (1986). Lives in the balance. On *Lives in the balance* [Record]. Los Angeles, CA: Asylum.

Buck, R., & Merchant, N. (1989). Please forgive us [Recorded by 10,000 Maniacs]. On *Blind man's 300* [Record]. Los Angeles, CA: Elektra.

Buckner, J., & Garcia, G. (1982). Pac-Man fever. On *Pac-Man fever* [Record]. New York, NY: Columbia.

Center for Gifted Education. (2007). *Guide to teaching social studies curriculum*. Dubuque, IA: Kendall Hunt.

Center for Gifted Education. (2011). *Autobiographies and memoirs*. Dubuque, IA: Kendall Hunt.

Cisneros, S. (1991). *The house on Mango Street*. New York, NY: Vintage. (Original work published in 1984)

Clancy, T. (2010). *The hunt for Red October*. New York, NY: Berkley. (Original work published in 1984)

Cockburn, B. (1984). Nicaragua. On *Stealing fire* [CD]. Ontario, Canada: True North.

Collins, P. (1989). Another day in paradise. On *. . . But seriously* [CD]. New York, NY: Atlantic.

Daniels, C., Crain, T., DiGregorio, T., Edwards, F., Marshall, J., & Hayward, C. (1980). In America [Recorded by The Charlie Daniels Band]. On *Full moon* [Record]. New York, NY: Epic.

DeYoung, D. (1983). Mr. Roboto [Recorded by Styx]. On *Kilroy was here* [Record]. Santa Monica, CA: A & M.

Downes, G., Horn, T., & Woolley, B. (1979). Video killed the radio star [Recorded by The Buggles]. On *The age of plastic* [Record]. London, England: Island.

Edelman, P. (2012, July 28). *Poverty in America: Why can't we end it?* Retrieved from http://www.nytimes.com/2012/07/29/opinion/Sunday/why-cant-we-end-poverty-in-america.html?pagewanted=all&_r=0

Fulghum, R. (2004). *All I really needed to know I learned in kindergarten*. New York, NY: Ballantine. (Original work published in 1988)

Gibson, B., Hopper, S., & Lewis, H. (1986). Hip to be square [Recorded by Huey Lewis and the News]. On *Fore!* [Record]. London, England: Chrysalis.

Greene, B. (1985, May 7). *An ambitious defense of yuppies*. Retrieved from http://articles. chicagotribune.com/1985-05-07/features/8501280315_1_yuppies-generation-hated

Greenwood, L. (1984). God bless the USA. On *You've got a good love comin'* [Record]. Nashville, TN: MCA.

Hazard, R. (1983). Girls just want to have fun [Recorded by Cyndi Lauper]. On *She's so unusual* [Record]. New York, NY: Epic.

Herbers, J. (1987, January 26). *Black poverty spreads in 50 biggest U.S. cities*. Retrieved from http:// www.nytimes.com/1987/01/26/us/black-poverty-spreads-in-50-biggest-us-cities.html

Hetfield, J., Burton, C., & Ulrich, L. (1984). Fight fire with fire [Recorded by Metallica]. On *Ride the lightning* [Record]. New York, NY: Megaforce.

Hudson, C., & Stevens, L. (1983). Holiday [Recorded by Madonna]. On *Madonna* [Record]. Los Angeles, CA: Sire.

Hues, J., Feldman, N., & Wolf, P. (1986). Everybody have fun tonight [Recorded by Wang Chung]. On *Mosaic* [CD]. Santa Monica, CA: Geffen.

Huntington, S. P. (2004). *Who are we? The challenges to America's national identity*. New York, NY: Simon and Schuster.

Jackson, J. (1984, July). *1984 Democratic National Convention address*. Speech presented at the 1984 Democratic National Convention, San Francisco, CA. Retrieved from http://www. americanrhetoric.com/speeches/jessejackson1984dnc.htm

Jackson, M. (1982a). Beat it. On *Thriller* [Record]. New York, NY: Epic.

Jackson, M. (1982b). Billie Jean. On *Thriller* [Record]. New York, NY: Epic.

Joel, B. (1982). Allentown. On *The nylon curtain* [Record]. New York, NY: Columbia.

Joel, B. (1989). Leningrad. On *Storm front* [CD]. New York, NY: Columbia.

John, E., & Taupin, B. (1985). Nikita [Recorded by Elton John]. On *Ice on fire* [CD]. London, England: Rocket.

Library of Congress. (n.d.). *Using primary sources*. Retrieved from http://www.loc.gov/teachers/ usingprimarysources/

Lopez, Y. (1984). *Things I never told my son about being a Mexican* [Multimedia artwork]. Retrieved from http://archive.newmuseum.org/index.php/Detail/Object/Show/object_id/3717

Lucas, R. (1983). Borderline [Recorded by Madonna]. Los Angeles, CA: Sire.

Madonna. (1983). Lucky star. On *Madonna* [Record]. Los Angeles, CA: Sire.

McAlea, K. (1984). 99 red balloons [Recorded by Nena]. On *Nena* [CD]. New York, NY: Columbia.

McKeague. P. M. (2009). *Writing about literature* (9th ed.). Dubuque, IA: Kendall Hunt.

Mellencamp, J. (1987). Down and out in paradise. On *The lonesome jubilee* [Record]. New York, NY: Mercury. (1986).

Mellencamp, J., & Green, G. (1987). Empty hands [Recorded by John Mellencamp]. On *The lonesome jubilee* [Record]. New York, NY: Mercury. (1986)

Merrill, G., & Rubicam, S. (1987). I wanna dance with somebody (who loves me) [Recorded by Whitney Houston]. On *Whitney* [CD]. New York, NY: Arista. (1986)

Michaels, B., DeVille, C. C., Dall, B., & Rockett, R. (1990). Something to believe in [Recorded by Poison]. On *Flesh & blood* [CD]. Torrance, CA: Enigma.

Min, Y. S. (1984). *Back of the bus 1953* [Drawing]. Retrieved from http://www.yongsoonmin.com/art/back-of-the-bus-1953/

Min, Y. S. (1989). *Make me* [Multimedia artwork]. Retrieved from http://www.yongsoonmin.com/art/make-me-all/

Morrison, T. (1983). *Recitatif.* Retrieved from http://nbu.bg/webs/amb/American/5/Morrison/recitatif.htm

Nasar, S. (1992, February 14). *Economic scene; puzzling poverty of the 80's boom.* Retrieved from http://www.nytimes.com/1992/02/14/business/economic-scene-puzzling-poverty-of-the-80-s-boom.html

National Governors Association Center for Best Practices, & Council of Chief State School Officers. (2010). *Common Core State Standards for English language arts and literacy in history/social studies, science, and technical subjects.* Washington, DC: Authors.

Peterik, J., & Sullivan, F. (1985). Burning heart [Recorded by Survivor]. On *Rocky IV soundtrack* [CD]. Los Angeles, CA: Sotti Bros.

Piesman, M., & Hartley, M. (1984). *The yuppie handbook: The state-of-the-art manual for young urban professionals.* New York, NY: Long Shadow Books.

Piper, A. (1986–1990). *My calling (cards) #1* [Printed art]. Retrieved from http://www.spencerart.ku.edu/exhibitions/radicalism/piper1.shtml

Prince. (1981). Ronnie, talk to Russia. On *Controversy* [Record]. Burbank, CA: Warner Bros.

Reagan, R. (1983, March). *Remarks at the Annual Convention of the National Association of Evangelicals.* Speech presented at the 41st Annual Convention of the National Association of Evangelicals, Orlando, FL. Retrieved from http://www.americanrhetoric.com/speeches/ronaldreaganevilempire.htm

Reagan, R. (1987, June). *Remarks on East-West relations at the Brandenburg Gate in West Berlin.* Berlin, Germany. Retrieved from http://www.reagan.utexas.edu/archives/speeches/1987/061287d.htm

Reid, V. (1989). Which way to America? [Recorded by Living Colour]. On *Vivid* [CD]. New York, NY: Epic. (1987–1988)

Reid, V., & Morris, T. (1989). Open letter (to a landlord) [Recorded by Living Colour]. On *Vivid* [CD]. New York, NY: Epic. (1987–1988)

Rew, K. (1983). Walking on sunshine [Recorded by Katrina and the Waves]. On *Walking on sunshine* [Record]. Toronto, Canada: Attic.

Ridenhour, C., Sadler, E., & Shocklee, H. (1987). Party for your right to fight [Recorded by Public Enemy]. On *It takes a nation of millions to hold us back* [Record]. New York, NY: Def Jam. (1987)

Ringgold, F. (1985). *Street story quilt part I, II, III* [Quilt]. Retrieved from http://metmuseum.org/toah/works-of-art/1990.237a-c

Rutherford, M., Banks, T., & Collins, P. (1986). Land of confusion [Recorded by Genesis]. On *Invisible touch* [Record]. London, England: Atlantic.

Rutherford, M., & Neil, C. (1991). Word of mouth [Recorded by Mike and the Mechanics]. On *Word of mouth* [CD]. London, England: Virgin.

Simmons, J., Smith, L., Simmons, R., & Hayden, D. (1984). Wake up [Recorded by Run–D.M.C.]. On *Run–D.M.C.* [Record]. New York, NY: Profile. (1983)

Smith, A. D. (2010). *National identity (Ethnonationalism comparative perspective).* Malden, MA: Polity Press.

Springsteen, B. (1985). My hometown. On *Born in the U.S.A.* [Record]. New York, NY: Columbia. (1983)

Sting. (1981). One world (not three) [Recorded by The Police]. On *Ghost in the machine* [Record]. Santa Monica, CA: A & M.

Taba, H. (1962). *Curriculum development: Theory and practice.* New York, NY: Harcourt Brace World.

Tan, A. (2006). *The joy luck club.* New York, NY: Penguin. (Original work published in 1989)

Temperton, R. (1982). Thriller [Recorded by Michael Jackson]. On *Thriller* [Record]. New York, NY: Epic.

Tennant, N., & Lowe, C. (1984). Opportunities (let's make lots of money) [Recorded by Pet Shop Boys]. On *Opportunities (let's make lots of money)* [Record]. London, England: Parlophone.

Wolfe, T. (2008). *The bonfire of the vanities.* New York, NY: Picador. (Original work published in 1987)

Yankovic, W. A. (1986). Christmas at ground zero. On *Polka party!* [Record]. Los Angeles, CA: Scott Bros.

APPENDIX

Unit Glossary

affluence: having much wealth, including money, property, and other material possessions

apartheid: a policy of racial segregation formerly practiced in the Republic of South Africa

assassination: the murder of a political figure, often by a surprise attack

coalition: a group of people who have joined together to achieve a common purpose

Cold War: The Cold War was a lengthy state of military and political tension between countries in the Western Bloc (the United States with NATO and others) and powers in the Eastern Bloc (the Soviet Union and its allies in the Warsaw Pact).

glasnost: a policy that called for increased openness and transparency in government activities in the Soviet Union

icon: a person regarded as a symbol of a cultural movement

immigrant: a person who comes from one country to live in another

inauguration: the official and ceremonial induction of a person into a government office

indigenous: native to a certain region or country

industry: the businesses that manufacture a certain product or provide a specific service

integrate: to combine something (often educational facilities or classes) that had been previously separated by race into one unified system

leisure: time when you are not working; free or unoccupied time

omnibus: including or relating to many items

perestroika: referred to the restructuring of the Soviet economic and political systems initiated by Mikhail Gorbachev in 1986

pop music: an abbreviation for "popular" music; refers to music of general appeal

protest: a display of disapproval in objection to something that one is powerless to prevent or avoid

Rust Belt: the heavily industrial area of the Northeastern United States that had many factories

sovereignty: independent power in government claimed by a certain group

technology: a machine or piece of equipment developed to solve problems or make a process more efficient

yuppie: stands for young, urban professional; referred to any young, college-educated city-dweller who had a professional career and made a substantial income

About the Authors

Molly Sandling is a teacher at Jamestown High School in Williamsburg, VA, where she teaches AP U.S. History and AP Human Geography. She completed her bachelor's degree in history at Yale University and her master's degree in education at the College of William and Mary, with an emphasis on adolescent social studies education. While in the master's degree program, she wrote the social studies units *The 1920s in America: A Decade of Tensions, The 1930s in America: Facing Depression, Defining Nations,* and *The Renaissance and Reformation in Europe* and received the NAGC Curriculum Award for *The 1920s in America.* Molly has been teaching since 2000, was the 2010 High School Teacher of the Year for Williamsburg-James City County Public Schools, and received National Board Certification in November 2012.

Kimberley Chandler, Ph.D., is the Curriculum Director at the Center for Gifted Education at the College of William and Mary and a clinical assistant professor. Kimberley completed her Ph.D. in Educational Policy, Planning, and Leadership with an emphasis in gifted education administration at the College of William and Mary. Her professional background includes teaching gifted students in a variety of settings, serving as an administrator of a school district gifted program, and providing professional development training for teachers and administrators nationally and internationally. Currently, Kimberley is the Network Representative on the NAGC Board of Directors and editor of the CEC-TAG newsletter *The Update.* Her research interests include curriculum policy and implementation issues in gifted programs, the design and evaluation of professional development programs for teachers of the gifted, and the role of principals in gifted education. Kimberley coauthored a book titled *Effective Curriculum for Underserved Gifted Students* and has served as the editor of many curriculum materials (science, social studies, language arts, and mathematics) from the Center for Gifted Education at The College of William and Mary.

Common Core State Standards Alignment

Grade Levels	Common Core State Standards in ELA-Literacy
K-12 College and Career Readiness Anchor Standards	L.CCRA.R.1: Read closely to determine what the text says explicitly and to make logical inferences from it; cite specific textual evidence when writing or speaking to support conclusions drawn from the text.
	L.CCRA.R.2: Determine central ideas or themes of a text and analyze their development; summarize the key supporting details and ideas.
	L.CCRA.R.4: Interpret words and phrases as they are used in a text, including determining technical, connotative, and figurative meanings, and analyze how specific word choices shape meaning or tone.
	L.CCRA.R.7: Integrate and evaluate content presented in diverse media and formats, including visually and quantitatively, as well as in words.
	L.CCRA.R.9: Analyze how two or more texts address similar themes or topics in order to build knowledge or to compare the approaches the authors take.
	L.CCRA.R.10: Read and comprehend complex literary and informational texts independently and proficiently.